THE GUINNESS BOOK OF SPORTING BLUNDERS

Cris Freddi

GUINNESS PUBLISHING

About the Author

A depressingly average footballer and tennis player, Cris Freddi is one of the best armchair sportsmen in Britain, appearing on BBC Radio's Brain of Sport and twice reaching the final of ITV's Sportsmasters.

The leading authority on matches played by the England football team, his England Football Fact Book was published by Guinness in 1991 and his articles appear regularly in the national press and specialist magazines.

Educated at Oxford, Cris is the author of two published novels and now lives in London.

Front cover: *Chris Waddle's missed penalty has cost England a place in the 1990 World Cup final. Lothar Matthäus sympathises but his eyes are on the trophy* (Photo: Bob Thomas Sports Photography)

Published in Great Britain by Guinness Publishing Ltd, 33 London Road, Enfield, Middlesex, UK

'Foot in Mouth' quotes courtesy of Private Eye's *Colemanballs.*

Designed by Cathy Shilling

Typeset in Garamond by Ace Filmsetting Ltd, Frome, Somerset

Printed and bound in Great Britain by The Bath Press, Bath, Avon

A catalogue record for this book is available from the British Library.
ISBN 0-85112-770-3

INTRODUCTION & ACKNOWLEDGEMENTS

The word that comes to mind is *glee*. The Germans have one too – *schadenfreude*, which is more precise – but glee's altogether more fun. Not joy, or delight, or contentment, but delicious pleasure in the mistakes of others, Unholy glee. Try saying it without grinning.

There's probably an element of debunking in there too. Watching the big fall hard. 'We always wanted to play like so-and-so. And now we do', that kind of thing.

We see sporting blunders all the time. TV's forever showing goalkeepers throwing the ball into their own net, boxers punching referees by mistake, etc. Generally speaking, I've kept to errors that actually *meant* something: dropped catches that cost entire Test series, missed penalties that lost cup finals, potted plants (yes, you read that right) which decided Olympic gold medals. In other words, only room for oops that led to an apocalypse.

I've also tried, where possible, to verify each incident (never let stories spoil a good fact). Everything in the book is correct (I hope) up to 1 June 1994. Any errors (!) are of course all my own work and nothing to do with the following folk, who helped with support and snippets of oddball information:

Steve Lynch, deputy editor of Wisden Cricket Monthly and mean quiz leaguer; Roger Titford, ace football quiz leaguer; George Church (ditto); the great Brian Mellowship as always; José Moretzsohn in Rio; John Barrett; Ronald R Milne (sub-librarian) and DE Coleman (deputy chief clerk) at Trinity College, Cambridge; Dr Janie Cottis, archivist at Magdalen College, Oxford; Julia Hore at Balliol College, Oxford; Nick Postma, secretary of Oxford City FC; the secretaries of Bishop Auckland FC, Kilmarnock FC, and St John's College, Oxford; the chairman of Leyton FC; Albert Sanders; AA Diment, secretary of Enfield FC; T Garner, director of Skelmersdale Utd FC; Harlequins RUFC; Len & Elsie Mellowship; Arianne Mortimer.

Above all, my editors at Guinness – Simon Duncan and Charles Richards – for planting the seed and making sure it grew without climbing the walls.

Grin and enjoy it. We did.

CONTENTS

CRASH COURSES

The third match in the 1907 series was the fifth rugby international so far between Australia and New Zealand. Australia had lost the first four but dominated the first hour in Sydney, only the covering of full-back 'General' Booth keeping the All Blacks in the game: 10 minutes from the end, they trailed only 5-0 when they relieved yet another Australian attack by kicking downfield.

The Australian full-back Dix went back to cover, gathered the ball – and collided with his captain Peter Burge, who'd had his eye on the ball to the exclusion of everything else. Now, a collision with 'Son' Burge meant something: at 14 stone he was the heaviest forward in the team. Dix dropped the ball, All Black centre Frank Mitchinson picked it up and ran in under the posts.

Billy Wallace's easy conversion drew the match 5-5, Australia lost the series 2-0 and had to wait another three years for their first win over New Zealand. Burge didn't play international rugby again.

In the 1930s, Hal Sever was probably the best winger in English rugby union. When Aleksandr Obolensky scored his two famous tries against the All Blacks in 1936, Sever (also winning his first cap) ran 35 yards for the third. A strong hard-running finisher, he scored five tries and dropped a winning goal in 10 internationals, winning a 1937 match by outsprinting half the Irish team and diving through a tackle at the corner.

The following year, he scored a try against Wales and was a constant threat against Ireland again: although he didn't score, England won 36-14 (worth 50-22 today). The third match of the season, against Scotland at Twickenham, was for the championship.

It went one way then the next, Renwick scoring a try for Scotland, Graham Parker putting England ahead with two penalty goals, Renwick going over again, Charlie Dick adding a third, Jim Unwin a first for England, Wilson Shaw a fourth for Scotland, who led 12-9 at half-time despite missing every kick at goal.

In the second half, their flanker WH Crawford at last got his sights right and put over two penalties for offside to regain the lead after Jeff Reynolds had dropped a goal. Parker kicked another penalty to bring the score back to 18-16 – then, in the last few minutes, England worked the ball down the line to Sever, who came inside and ran in for the winning try.

Ran into, to be exact. The goalpost, that is. Smack bang, the ball went loose, Sever's teeth followed suit, Scotland got the ball away. In the last minute, Shaw scored a famous individualistic try to clinch the match 21-16 and give Scotland their last Triple

Foot in mouth
"Shaun Edwards has happy memories of Wembley. On his last appearance here, he received a fractured cheekbone."
RAY FRENCH

In 1941, Swedish speed skater Ake Seyffarth set a world record of 8 mins 13.7 for the 5000 metres. At the 1948 Olympics, he was closing in on the gold medal when he brushed against a photographer who'd wandered onto the ice to take his picture!

The collision cost Seyffarth several seconds, the difference between the gold (won in a time almost 16 seconds slower than his world record) and the 8th place he had to settle for.

Seyffarth went on to win silver in the 1500 and gold in the 10 000.

Crown before 1984. It was the last post for Harold Sedgewick Sever, who didn't play for England again.

In 1956, another over-eager photographer (*see left*) decided the destination of an Oympic gold medal. Near the end of the 7th lap of the cycling road race, the British team of Alan Jackson, Arthur Brittain and Bill Holmes were looking set for gold. Then a woman photographer stepped out for a closer shot – and didn't leave Holmes enough time to avoid her.

As well being badly injured, Holmes lost two minutes in changing his damaged wheel, more than enough to cost Britain the gold. He caught up with the other two 11 miles later, but France took the race by a single point. Had the British finished just one second faster, they would have won it instead.

Vic Elford of Britain won the 1968 Monte Carlo Rally and might well have done it again the following year. Leading the race with three stages to go, he crashed into a tree *after* one of the finishing lines! He didn't win the race again.

In December 1981, a familiar figure was padding through the streets of Hove on a training run when news of a carol service on a church noticeboard caught his eye. The figure didn't look across for long (he moved pretty quickly in those days) but the distraction changed the shape of things to come, not least the figure's leg.

Someone, it seems, was moving in mysterious ways. While the figure was glancing at the church, the church was running into the figure, who fell over the railings, which punctured a thigh muscle, ruptured some ligaments, and kept the figure out of the two main athletics championships in 1982 as well as a lucrative challenge race or races against a famous rival who's now a parliamentary figure.

The injuries healed, but the facts of the figure were drastically affected: boxed in during the 1983 world championship final, terrible bronchial trouble in the 1984 Olympics, gold in a diluted Commonwealth 5000 in 1986, 10th in the same event at the 1987 worlds, tears after a fuss about AAA participation money.

Currently a prominent figure in ITV's athletics coverage, he's slower than in his prime but can now run faster than a church.

Foot in mouth
"Those days of Stirling Moss seem to be gone for ever, and long may they continue."
WILLIAM
WOOLLARD

The finish of the 1984 Olympic modern pentathlon was the closest ever. At the very end of the last event, the 4000 metres cross-country, the favourite, 1982 world champion Daniele Masala of Italy, was passed by Svante Rasmuson of Sweden, who only had to stay upright for the last 100 metres to win the gold medal he'd missed four years earlier (he'd finished fourth in Moscow).

Once Pascal Simon had taken the yellow jersey, he seemed to have the 1983 Tour de France sewn up: a lead of 4 mins 22 secs and the mountains to come (he was a renowned climber).

Then, in trying to avoid the three riders who were protecting their Portuguese leader Joaquim de Agostinho, he moved too far to one side, collided with a motorcycle outrider (there to protect riders from the public!) and joined him in a roadside ditch.

Simon carried on for several days despite a triple hairline fracture of the shoulderblade, but eventually had to bow to the inevitable, retire, and allow Laurent Fignon to win the Tour for the first of two years in a row. Simon didn't win it once.

Only 20 yards from the end of four days' effort, Rasmuson rounded the last turn, skidded, recovered his balance – and oops a daisy. Oops some kind of flower, anyway. He fell over a potted plant that the organisers had installed to decorate the course!

Masala passed him, won the gold, and added another in the team event. Rasmuson, who finished only 13 points behind, never came so close to an Olympic title again.

British 10 000 metre runner Carl Thackeray, selected for the 1991 world championships, never got there. Out training in New Mexico, he ran into a cactus! His place in Britain's team was taken by Andy Bristow.

England's 1992 sweet chariot, after running over Scotland 25-7 away and Ireland 38-9 at Twickenham, didn't expect to be stopped in Paris (where they hadn't lost since 1988) on the way to a second successive Grand Slam.

At half-time, thanks to a penalty try and another by full-back Jonathan Webb, they led 15-4. An exchange of penalties made it 18-7, then the French, with time running out, tried a scissors move in midfield.

Fly-half Alain Penaud collided with substitute Jean-Luc Sadourny, the ball went loose, Will Carling picked it up, scrum-half Dewi Morris moved it on, Rory Underwood went over for a try, England led 22-7 and the match was over.

Soon afterwards, Penaud scored a try after charging down Will Carling's swanky kick, but it was too late for amends. England went 27-13 ahead before Irish referee Stephen Hilditch sent off two of the French front row: Grégoire Lascubé for stamping on Martin Bayfield, Vincent Moscato for butting Jeff Probyn. Morris scored a fourth try, England won 31-13 and went on to win Grand Slam II by beating Wales 24-0 at Twickenham.

And one near miss

During the 1924 rugby league Challenge Cup final, a mounted policeman got in the way of Wigan's Adrian van Heerden. The South African winger sidestepped the English horse to score a try, Wigan beat Oldham 21-4.

FALL GUYS

and fall gals

Speed skaters fall down quite a lot. It looks difficult to keep your feet when they're standing on thin blades and you've got thighs like baby trees. Even in the Olympics.

In the re-run of the 1932 1500 metre final, Herbert Taylor of the USA was in the lead coming round the last bend, then skidded across the ice and fell into a bank of snow. He finished 8th and never won an Olympic medal.

In the 1972 Games, the mighty Dutchman Ard Schenk, overall world champion three years in a row, won all the men's events except one, the shortest. Pushing off at the start of the 500 metres, he managed only four steps before falling over and finishing 34th.

A week before the 1988 Olympics, Dan Jansen of the States won the world sprint title to set himself up as favourite for the 500 metres. After a false start, he was away well enough, only to fall at the very first bend. Four days later, in the 1000 metres, he fell over again. In 1994, by now the world record holder, he slipped during the 500 and finished 8th, only 0.35 sec behind the winner.

In the last race of his fourth Games, the 1994 1000m, he set another world record in winning the gold, his only Olympic medal.

Below: *The thought of having to wait another six years gets Dan Jansen down* (Popperfoto)

Foot in mouth

"The almost unknown Kenyan came here with a big reputation."
DAVID COLEMAN

Harrison 'Bones' Dillard, who'd been given the track shoes which won Jesse Owens four Olympic golds in 1936, went to the 1948 AAU meeting at Milwaukee unbeaten in his last 82 races (hurdles and sprints, indoors and out) but succumbed to an archaic system that forced him to race four times in just over an hour, losing to Norwood 'Barney' Ewell in the 100 yards and Bill Porter in the high hurdles.

Nevertheless he was the big favourite for the latter in the Olympic trials the following week. Away well at the start, he hit the first hurdle, a shock in itself for such a purist, lost his stride, hit another hurdle, then another, then stopped, rhythm all gone, in front of the seventh: the biggest shock omission from the Olympic team.

The rest is all too well known. He'd qualified in third place for the 100 metres, went on to win the gold medal at Wembley, added another in the relay, made the hurdles team four years later, won that gold too, and yet another in the relay: as many, all told, as Owens himself.

Leading in the last few yards of the 1970 Commonwealth Games 1500 metres, Sylvia Potts of New Zealand needed only to keep her feet to win the gold medal. Instead, she lost them completely, fell just before the line, and picked herself up just in time to see virtually the whole field go by. Rita Ridley of England won her only major international title, Potts finished eighth in the event four years later and never won a Commonwealth medal.

In the same Games, hot favourite Kerry O'Brien of Australia fell at the water jump during the 3000m steeplechase final and had to drop out, allowing his team mate Tony Manning to win the race by 20 yards. Two years later, still the world record holder, O'Brien fell at the water jump again and didn't make the Olympic final.

With 300 metres to go in the 1976 Olympic steeplechase final, Anders Garderud of Sweden, the world record holder who'd never won a major championship, overtook his perennial rival Bronislaw Malinowski of Poland and opened up a gap of five yards at the water jump. At last a gold medal for the eternal under-achiever.

Then, as the Swede gathered himself for the last hurdle, the young East German Frank Baumgartl appeared in his rear view mirror, full of running and accelerating with every step.

Garderud desperately cleared the last hurdle but had no sprint finish left. Baumgartl did, but never got to use it. He smacked the hurdle with his trailing knee, fell, got up, and finished third behind Malinowski, who'd had to jump over him. Garderud set his fourth world record in winning that elusive gold medal, Malinowski won it four years later, Baumgartl was never heard of again.

On the last lap of the first world championship steeplechase final, at Helsinki in 1983, two fast finishers made their move, little Patriz Ilg of West Germany scooting past Mariano Scartezzini and Boguslaw Maminski, bigger Henry Marsh of the USA picking up speed in fourth.

Into the home straight, Marsh went past Maminski and began to close on Ilg. But the Mormon's eccentric tactics (he spent the bulk of his races at the very back then made preposterously long runs for home) were too exhausting for success at the highest level. At the last barrier, too tired to get his leg over, he fell and could only finish eighth, letting Colin Reitz of Great Britain in for the bronze.

Ilg added the world title to his European gold; Marsh never learned. The following year, again the favourite, yet again leaving it much too late, he finished fourth in the Olympics, falling over at the line.

Left: *Henry Marsh lies back and thinks of England's Colin Reitz, who takes the bronze at Helsinki* (Popperfoto)

After winning his first major title at 400m hurdles, the 1974 Commonwealth, Alan Pascoe set off on his lap of honour. Naturally the hurdles were still in place, and one of them stood in his way as he trotted back down the home straight.

Now, a hurdle is a hurdle is a hurdle, and if you're a hurdler you hurdle hurdles, which is what Pascoe tried to do to this one, even though a) he'd just raced the strength out of his legs, and b) it was facing the wrong way.

He hit it, it hit back, and he ended up with his spine bent across it and the crowd enjoying the spectacle he'd made of himself. In the best traditions of those who get straight back on a horse or bike after falling off, he tried again – and collapsed in another heap. More spectatorial merriment.

Pascoe cleared the hostile inanimate object at the third attempt, but by then his reputation had been established. The hurdle scraped the skin off his lower back (which made his next hot shower interesting) and the British Sports Photographers Association presented him with a framed shot of the incident. He won two European Championship golds later in the year.

Soon after the 1988 Olympics, Gail Devers began feeling chronically ill and her body started behaving very strangely. She went from 8st 2 to 9st 9 in two weeks and her hair began to fall out. She suffered memory loss, migraines, and sporadic loss of vision in one eye. Her body shook involuntarily and four menstrual cycles per month left her with a dreadful loss of blood. She developed blood blisters on her feet and had to train in five pairs of socks to cushion her against the pain. Her feet swelled to an astonishing Size 11 and began to bleed, then secrete pus: she came within days of having them both amputated.

Eventually she was diagnosed as suffering from Graves' Disease, a rare thyroid condition which required radiation therapy – but not until her podiatrist had spent all that time diagnosing athlete's foot!

Within months of having her therapy changed, she was proving she had athlete's feet, winning silver in the 100m hurdles at the world championships.

At the Olympics the following year, she won a shock gold medal in the 100 metres flat, and became the clear favourite for the hurdles when Lyudmila Narozhilenko, who'd beaten her in the world championships, pulled a hamstring before the semis.

In the final, Devers led by three yards coming to the last flight – but she was going too fast for her own good, hit the hurdle hard, and staggered over the line in 5th place behind the virtually unknown Paraskevi (Voula) Patoulidou, who became the first Greek Olympic gold medallist since 1912.

The following year, Devers got her stride pattern right to win the world title in the hurdles as well as the flat.

LEFT? RIGHT? WRONG

taking the wrong direction

When Jim Corkery of Canada came into Stamford Bridge stadium at the end of the 1912 Polytechnic Marathon, he turned the wrong way. He still won the race, but the extra 360 yards he ran deprived him of a new world record.

At the 40 km mark in the 1954 European championship Marathon, three men were running together: Boris Grishyayev and Ivan Filin of the USSR, and Veikko Karvonen of Finland. Less than a mile from the finish, Filin accelerated away to a certain win as Karvonen settled for his second successive silver in the event.

Inside the stadium itself, Filin put in his finishing sprint – in the wrong direction. The 100 yards he lost were enough to push him back to third as Karvonen took the gold. Four years later, Filin won the silver.

In 1966, Jim Alder of Scotland also went the wrong way at the end

Below: *On home ground, and going the right way this time, Jim Alder finishes only second in 1970* (Popperfoto)

9

Donald Healey should have won the 1928 Monte Carlo Rally. Having worked his way through Germany, Belgium and France, he had time in hand when he reached Fréjus, but turned along the wrong road from Nice and lost the whole race by just two minutes.

of a major championship Marathon, on the outskirts of the Commonwealth Games stadium, but was strong enough to recover and beat Bill Adcocks for the gold. In 1970 he won the silver in Edinburgh.

Just how old was boxer Jersey Joe Walcott when he won the world heavyweight title at last? Officially, 37 years 168 days – but some say 40 or more. Whatever, he was the oldest ever and one of the most respected, a fighters' fighter who could take as well as dish out.

Nevertheless he was very much the underdog for his second defence, at Philadelphia in September 1952. Rocky Marciano, no spring chicken himself but nine years younger, had won every one of his 42 pro fights, 37 by a knockout. Jersey Joe's record, in contrast, included 15 defeats in 64 bouts. At the age of 38 (and the rest) he wasn't expected to last the distance.

Marciano almost didn't last the first round. After less than a minute, he walked onto a left hook and went down for the first time in his career. By the end of the round, his lip was bleeding and he could barely see out of his left eye.

For the next eleven rounds, all the old misgivings about Marciano seemed to be being proved right. You'll never be a fighter, he'd been told. You'll be too heavy for a light-heavyweight and too light for a heavyweight. You're too old to be starting out (23). You're not tall enough. Your arms are way too short and your legs are too thick. You'll get murdered in the pros.

Instead, it was the pros who got killed (almost literally in Carmine Vingo's case) – but here in the title fight he was being jabbed to pieces. Cut on the bridge of the nose, cut just above what was left of his hairline, cut under the eye, he needed 14 stitches afterwards.

As if that wasn't enough, his eyes were burning from something on his trainer's sponge (or, it was claimed, the champion's gloves) and only the bell saved him at the end of the 12th. Walcott may have been ancient, but he was two inches taller, ten pounds heavier, and had a seven-inch advantage in reach. It was a slaughter.

In the 13th, a mile ahead on points, Jersey Joe backed away when Marciano threw a left to the body, waited for the bleeding bull to come in yet again, stabbed him with jabs – then, when the Rock was too close to keep off, sidestepped away along the ropes. He only had to go the same way as the next right hand to minimise its impact. Instead he went to the left.

Photographs of the impact never get any prettier. Jersey Joe's face was contorted by the punch he moved into, the spray of sweat went up, he fell on one knee with his left arm hooked over the middle rope and his head on the floor. The referee, Charley Daggert, could have counted to a hundred.

Not surprisingly, Walcott was never the same again. The following May, no longer Jersey Joe but just 39-year-old Arnold Raymond Cream who'd gone on one fight too many, he occupied Marciano for less than a round then retired. The Rock, whose arms and legs never got any longer but whose heart stayed as big as himself, was still champion when he retired in 1956, unbeaten in 49 fights. Careful with his well-being as well as his money, he wasn't tempted by the half-century.

When the Minnesota Vikings defensive end Jim Marshall picked up a fumble by the San Francisco 49ers in 1964, he saw the chance to run with the ball, hold off all challenges in a 66-yard dash, and touch down in the end zone – for a safety, worth two points to the 49ers. He'd been running the wrong way!

Great stuff, but the Vikings still won (27-22) – so the palm in this category has to go to the immortal Ron Riegels.

In the 1929 Rose Bowl, the big college game of the season, California centre Riegels picked up a fumble on the Georgia Tech 20-yard line and made for the end zone. The wrong one, at the far end of the stadium.

Eventually one of his team mates, Benny Lom, realised what was happening and set off in pursuit. Riegels saw him coming and gritted his teeth. Lom pinned back his ears. Yard by yard, the two athletes battled it out, neither giving an inch. Finally, just a yard from their own line, Lom's tackle brought Riegels back to earth.

On the next play, Lom's (understandably weary) kick was charged down for the two-point safety that cost California the title 8-7.

Riegels, who explained that he'd been egged on by the noise of the crowd, who he thought were encouraging him, was rewarded with a proposal of marriage in which the couple would walk the wrong way along the aisle, and a variety of sponsorship ideas: upside-down cakes, clocks with hands that went backwards (you get the picture).

Going into the 1964 Mexican Grand Prix, Graham Hill had to do no more than stay on the track to regain the Formula One world title.

On Lap 30, he approached a banked hairpin which required careful consideration. Make the wrong decision and you could find yourself thrown up onto the top of the banking. Hill took the inside line – and lost everything. Colliding with Lorenzo Bandini, he rammed his guard rail backwards, which more or less closed

Foot in mouth
"Mansell is almost metaphorically in sight of the chequered flag."
MURRAY WALKER

his exhaust pipes together and forced him into the pits.

He rejoined the race, but knew that unless both Jim Clark and John Surtees retired, the championship was gone. Clark's oil pipe broke with only two laps to go, but Surtees became the only man to win overall world titles on four wheels as well as two when Bandini let him through on Ferrari team orders. He beat Hill by a single point.

Four years later, on the same course, at exactly the same corner, Hill tangled with Pedro Rodriguez, charging round in front of his home crowd, survived, and won the title.

When Tony Greig picked the team for his first Test as England cricket captain, he surprised a few (though not the county professionals) by including the grey-haired, bespectacled Northants No. 3 David Steele, whose international chance seemed to have passed him by (he was nearly 34).

Greig, winning his first toss, chose to bat in the face of Lillee and Thomson. Within minutes, England were 10-1 and Steele on his way out to the middle.

He'd come out to bat at Lord's any number of times, but of course always from the visitors' changing room. Now he went down a flight of stairs, thought about it, went down another – and found himself in the toilet.

He didn't sink so low again that summer. Once he'd explored his way out of the pavilion, he made exactly 50 in his first Test innings, shared a stand of 96 with Greig, headed the England averages with 365 runs at 60.83, and was voted BBC Sports Personality of the Year.

At the end of the fifth stage of the 1978 Tour de France, Jan Raas sprinted away to a certain win – so fast that he missed a curve and landed in the crowd. He finished 24th overall.

TOO EARLY BIRDS

making the move too soon

Three golfers tied for first place in the 1940 US Open. Two took part in a play-off for the title, Lawson Little beating the great Gene Sarazen. The third, despite everyone's best efforts, had to be disqualified.

When they saw the weather taking a turn for the worse, six players rushed to get their rounds in before the rain came. At the first tee, they found only an unofficial scorer, a single marshall, and a handful of journalists (the USPGA's executive secretary Joe Dey was having the lunch he was entitled to).

The marshall explained that the players had to start at their allotted times and not before, but they insisted. Even when two reporters, Merrell Whittlesey of the Washington Post and Maury Fitzgerald of the Washington Times Herald, told them about another player who'd been disqualified for starting out of turn, the six wouldn't listen. They teed off, completed their rounds, and were thrown out of the tournament.

For one in particular it was costly beyond all proportion. Ed Oliver junior, whose nickname (Porky) said much about his shape but nothing about his talent (for golf, at least) was barred from the play-off, despite the protests of Little and Sarazen.

Ed Porky finished eighth in the US Open in 1946 (two strokes off the lead) and fourth in 1947 (three shots adrift). He never won a Major.

Hard to imagine any athlete falling further and faster from grace than poor Ray Norton in 1960. Co-holder of the world record in the 200 metres, and in the 100 until just before the Olympics, he went to Rome as favourite for the track sprint treble.

In the final of the 100, he couldn't match Armin Hary's blitz start, or Dave Sime's finish, or anyone else's anything, and finished last. In the 200, he was in the lead until the last 20 yards of the final, then went backwards. Last again.

Still, there was always the sprint relay to come, an event the USA hadn't failed to win since the very first, in 1912. Although the Germans equalled the world record in the heats, the Americans were expected to win, even when Frank Budd could finish only fourth on the first leg. Their fancied runners were still to come.

The first was Otis Ray Norton. Anxious to make up for his individual failures, he shot away on the second leg – much too soon. Budd shouted at him but it was too late. By the time Norton received the baton he was three yards beyond the changeover zone and almost standing still. He ran a strong race, pulling the

Foot in mouth
"There's no excuse for pace."
ALEX MURPHY

Before the England v New Zealand rugby match at Twickenham in 1964, both teams were called off the pitch before the start, but the marching band misunderstood, came off themselves, and didn't return. It was the only time the national anthems weren't played before an international at Twickenham.

13

After winning three Grands Prix in 1958 with Vanwall, the talented young British driver Tony Brooks was signed by Ferrari, who took him to the verge of the world title itself.

In 1959, after winning two more races, he went into the last of the championship, the US Grand Prix at Sebring in Florida, with a real chance of beating Jack Brabham to the overall title. On the very first lap, his team mate Wolfgang von Trips clipped his rear wheel.

It was no more than a nudge in the back, and Brooks should have ignored it, or at worst waited to see if anything developed. Instead, far too hastily, he went into the pits.

There was nothing wrong with the car. He rejoined the race but could finish only third, losing the title to Brabham, who got out and pushed his car home in fourth place. Brooks, who didn't win another Grand Prix, retired in 1961 at the early age of 29.

team up to second, and Sime's anchor leg took them past the Germans virtually on the line.

All to no avail. The inevitable disqualification sent Otis Ray home in triple disgrace.

In 1988, as always, the USA were favourites for the same event. This time they didn't even make the final. In the qualifying heat, reserve runner Lee McNeill went off spectacularly early and didn't take the baton from Calvin Smith until he was five yards beyond the zone. McNeill never won an Olympic medal, Smith won one gold instead of two, Carl Lewis eight instead of nine.

The USA have failed to win the men's Olympic sprint relay only four times – and never on merit, as it were: once as the result of a boycott (1980), three times by disqualification (1912, 1960, 1988).

Britain, having won the men's European Cup for the first time (at Gateshead in 1989) would have retained it in Frankfurt two years later if the sprint relay had played it safe.

Instead, looking for revenge over the French quartet which had set a world record in beating them to the European title the previous year, they went for broke, passing the baton on the limit of the zone.

At the last changeover, Linford Christie went off too quickly ahead of Marcus Adam, whose look of dismay said it all as Christie sprinted home. The disqualification (and loss of all points from the event) left the rest of the team too much to do on the second day.

Before winning the track 5000/10 000m double at the 1977 and 1979 World Cups and 1980 Olympics, Miruts Yifter had had to pay some dues, by missing the start of the 1972 Olympic 5000 (see THE IMPORTANT THING . . .) and, before that, in the 1971 USA v Africa match.

The day before winning the 10 000, he should have won the five. After tracking the fans' favourite Steve Prefontaine through the closing stages, he gave the world its first look at his remarkable finishing kick – a lap too soon.

Exhausted, he could only shuffle round as Prefontaine won the race.

In the controversial, risible world of race walking, Mikhail Shchennikov's been virtually unbeatable indoors, gold medallist at the last four world championships, three times European champion.

In the open air, it's been a different matter. Lugano Cup winner

1991, but no golds in Olympics, European or world champion-ships. He missed his best chance at the 1991 worlds in Tokyo.

In the last stages of the 20km, he vied for the lead with Daniel Plaza and defending champion Maurizio Damilano. Coming into the stadium, he accelerated away to cross the line first – only to realise that there was another lap to go (no fault of the officials, all his own work).

Tired by his finishing burst, he couldn't hold Damilano, who retained the title by fifty yards.

In 1974, Eddie Merckx won the Tour de France for the fifth time to equal Jacques Anquetil's record. The following year, despite keeping the yellow jersey for two weeks, he led Bernard Thevenet by less than a minute and decided to make a telling move between Nice and the ski resort of Pra-Loup, a stage with two climbs of over 7000 feet, surely more than enough to drop Thevenet, who didn't enjoy long steep descents.

As planned, Merckx was first to each of the great summits, but he'd made his move too soon. Even though he increased his lead on the last descent, he'd run out of juice. With 20 kilometres still to go before Pra-Loup, he was a pitiable sight. Felice Gimondi, the 1965 Tour winner, tried to help him along but it was useless. Thevenet, who finished the stage with an overall lead as long as the deficit with which he'd started it (58 seconds), won the Tour, and regained it two years later. Merckx had to be content with a share of the record number of wins.

So did Bernard Hinault, who had two chances of that sixth success. In 1984, after missing the previous year's Tour, under pressure from holder Laurent Fignon's suspiciously tireless riding, he went for broke on the shortish stage from Grenoble to the infamous Alpe d'Huez.

His first attack, on the second of the three climbs, the sheer face of the Côte de Laffrey, didn't work. Five riders went with him, including the aquiline Scot Robert Millar, Pedro Delgado, and Fignon himself, who counter-attacked near the summit.

Hinault gave chase, caught Fignon in the valley just before the terrifying Alpe, and looked set to win the stage. Then, instead of taking a breather and attacking again on the mountain itself, he went off in front. On his own. Into the wind.

An incredible blunder from such a giant. It's said that Fignon laughed out loud when it happened. Hinault, exhausted even before the higher slopes of the Alpe, finished three minutes behind Fignon, who won the Tour for the second successive year.

Another prominent middle-distance runner made the same mistake as Yifter in 1985. Running in the first women's 10 000 metre race to be included in the World Cup, tiny Olga Bondarenko sprinted away to finish well ahead of the field – again a lap too early. Head down, she struggled on – but Aurora Cunha of Portugal won the race.

The following year, Bondarenko won the European title at 3000 metres, then beat Liz McColgan to win the 1988 Olympic 10 000.

Above: *Eyes on the prize.*
While Hinault (right) goes
too soon on the Alpe d'Huez,
LeMond follows his star
(Popperfoto)

Hinault, nothing daunted, came back to win it the following year for the fifth time, and was the favourite in 1986, when another hasty move wrecked his last chance.

Still tired after taking the overall lead at Pau the day before, he nevertheless elected to attack on the descent of the famous Tourmalet. This with three intimidating climbs still to come: Aspin, Peyresourde, finally the dreaded Super-Bagnères.

It would have been risky at the best of times. In this heat, after his exertions of the previous day, and with seven mountain goats for company (Millar, Urs Zimmermann of Switzerland, and no fewer than five Colombians), it was sheer bravado.

By the time his team mate Greg Lemond reached him, Hinault was in a bad way. The American, still playing the loyal *domestique*, asked his team leader if he wanted any help. No point, said Hinault to his credit, I'm finished. Lemond stormed away to recoup everything he'd lost the day before.

Even after this, Hinault didn't hold back. For the second time, the Alpe d'Huez cost him the Tour. Again pressing too hard and too early, he finished five minutes ahead of the pack – but with Lemond in tow. The effort took so much out of him that he couldn't go with Zimmermann's attack on the Granon. Lemond, who could, became the first American to win the Tour.

TOO LATE BIRDS

not making it soon enough

In a rugby international at Newport in 1884, Wales half-back Harry Gwynn, a brilliant runner and handler given to famous lapses, dummied the Scottish defence, dashed through the gap he'd made, carried the ball over the Scotland line – then, instead of simply touching down for the try, looked round for someone to pass to!

No-one there except Scottish defenders. Gwynn lost the ball, Wales the match by a try and dropped goal to nil.

At Leeds in 1896, England made a late dash to save the game against Ireland. Clever interpassing on the left between EM (Edward Morgan) Baker and EF (Ernest Faber) Fookes ended in the latter going over under the posts – then running on too far and ending up out of play beyond the dead-ball line. Ireland survived 10-4 to win the championship.

At Twickenham in 1985, a substandard England team did its best to hold out against France, but couldn't stop the move that sent Patrick Estève in for a try in the left corner.

Estève, a fast, rather straightforward winger who'd scored a try in every match of the 1983 championship, looked certain to touch down for another here. He actually crossed the line – then, trying to work his way closer to the posts (though it looked as if he were simply rubbing English noses in it), he allowed the tenacious little 31-year-old scrum-half Richard Harding to flap at the ball in his hands, finally to knock it away.

The missed try made all the difference. England held out for a 9-9 draw and France missed a share in the championship by a single point.

Below: *The fall after the pride: Estève caught short by Harding (9). A young Rory Underwood learns how not to do it* (Colorsport)

Foot in mouth

"We've said it once, we've said it many times: there's no excuse for pace."
ALEX MURPHY

For more than a decade, Raymond Poulidor was France's favourite cyclist (*Poupou tu es le papa*) and runner-up. Three times he finished second overall in the Tour de France, four times third, without winning it or ever wearing the yellow jersey.

His rivalry with Jacques Anquetil was the main theme of the Sixties. By the time Poulidor entered his first Tour, in 1962, he was 25, and the shrewd pragmatic Anquetil, less of a late developer, had already won the event twice. No match for Poulidor in the mountains (*Poulidor le plus fort*), he was unbeatable in time trials, which did nothing to capture the French public's imagination but went a long way towards winning the Tour five times.

In 1964, the peasant Poulidor came closest to knocking Seigneur Anquetil off his seat, riding shoulder to shoulder with him up the fearsome Puy de Dôme, reducing the overall lead to 14 seconds, losing the whole thing by only 55.

The following year, Poulidor had every opportunity, but even in Anquetil's absence he couldn't take them, finishing second to Felice Gimondi, who was taking part in the Tour for the first time.

In 1968, with Anquetil way past his peak, Poulidor had his best chance of all. With the holder Roger Pingeon riding as his virtual assistant and no-one else posing any kind of threat, the whole of France waited for Poupou to make his move. And waited. Not for the last half of a time trial, or an entire stage, but for more than two weeks. Finally, Pingeon ran out of patience and set off himself, Poulidor gave chase, crashed into a motorcycle outrider and out of the Tour. He never came close again.

In 1986, Dancing Brave was beyond question the best Classic horse in Europe, winner of the 2000 Guineas and Eclipse Stakes. However, before the Derby he'd never been tested over a mile and a half, even in training, so it was no surprise that Greville Starkey should play a waiting game on him. The mistake was in letting the game go on too long.

Not only that, but Starkey found it hard to handle Epsom's peculiar bumps and humps and took too long to get Dancing Brave balanced. By the time he did, and moved him to the wide outside, he was ten lengths off the lead with only two furlongs to go.

Even then, the colt was so good he almost got there. On level ground at last, he settled down and charged past everyone except Walter Swinburn on Shahrastani, who held him off by only half a length.

Starkey's misjudgment cost him the ride in the King George VI & Queen Elizabeth and the Arc de Triomphe, in which Pat Eddery rode the Brave to victory ahead of Shahrastani each time.

TOO GOOD FOR THEIR OWN GOOD

Gloucestershire and England slow left-armer Charlie Parker took 9-36 against Yorkshire in 1922, including a hat-trick (he hit the stumps with five consecutive deliveries, the second a no-ball), doing himself no favours in the process: he lost valuable gate money by shortening his own benefit match.

Back in 1907, the mighty Middlesex all-rounder Albert Trott, who played Test cricket for both Australia and England and was the only batsman to hit a ball over the Lord's pavilion, had gone one better, if that's the word.

In his benefit match against Somerset, he took four wickets in five balls, two hat-tricks in the same innings, and finished the match a day early: 'I'm bowling myself into the workhouse.'

When the Rev. David Sheppard was recalled for England's 1962–63 tour of Australia, he was short of practice, especially fielding practice. A series of dropped catches made him the butt of Fred Trueman's sledgehammer wit: 'Pretend it's Sunday, Reverend, and keep your hands together.'

During the match with Victoria, he ran round the boundary to get under a pull from Test opener Bill Lawry, got his hands to it, and surprised everyone by holding on.

It was a no-ball. While Sheppard was retrieving the ball he'd thrown up in delight, the batsmen ran an extra run.

In the absence of the great professionals (Gonzales, Rosewall, Laver) Roy Emerson was the world's best tennis player in the mid Sixties, winner of 11 Grand Slam singles titles, still the most by any male player. In 1966 he was No. 1 seed and unquestioned favourite to become the first man since Fred Perry to win the Wimbledon title for a third successive year. In the quarter-final against fellow Australian Owen Davidson, a left-handed doubles specialist, he won the first set 6-1.

When Davidson played a short angled ball that barely cleared the net, there seemed to be no danger. That's to say, most players would have left it and conceded the point. But Emmo, at his peak, was the fittest and fastest player around. Head down, he chased the shot, reached it, couldn't control it, or himself, slipped, and crashed into the umpire's chair. Davidson took the next three sets and Emerson didn't win the Wimbledon singles title again.

Foot in mouth
"They are still faster, although their times are the same."
DAVID COLEMAN

Foot in mouth

"Hagi has probably been the best player on the field. Without any question."
BOBBY CHARLTON

American football does it more socialistically than English soccer. The team with the worst record in the NFL has first pick of the best college players for the following year, the second-worst team has second go, etc. It sometimes works.

In 1968 three teams were vying for bottom spot, which was the place to be that season. The prize for rear of the year was the great running back Orenthal James Simpson, the famous OJ, winner of the Heisman Trophy as best college player of the year.

When the Philadelphia Eagles lost their first 11 games, they looked favourites for Simpson's signature. But the Pittsburgh Steelers (who'd lost 11 while winning only two) and the Buffalo Bills were still in the frame.

The Steelers tried to lose to the Eagles but couldn't. With Pittsburgh out of the running, Philadelphia needed to lose two of their last three games but contrived to win two and lost OJ to the Bills. Disgruntled Eagles fans began a Joe Must Go campaign against general Joe Kuharich!

During the 1975 Ashes series in England, the big Australian medium-pacer Max Walker chased a ball down to the longest part of the boundary, stopped it just inside, went over the rope himself, came back, picked the ball up and threw it in, saving the four. The batsmen ran five.

Although the West Indies came back shell-shocked from Australia, where they'd lost the 1975–76 series 5-1, they were expected to have little trouble with India at home, especially after winning the first Test by an innings.

Even when the Indians came within two wickets of winning the second, no alarms sounded. In the third, after taking a first innings lead of 131, Clive Lloyd declared at 271-6 to set India a target of 403. Only one other team had scored 400 runs to win a Test, and that had had Bradman in it.

But now the West Indian spinners bowled like drains. Lloyd had accepted three in the team – Albert Padmore, Raphick Jumadeen, Imtiaz Ali – because the match was played on the traditional Trinidad turner, but he hadn't been entirely convinced.

One way or another, he was now. Jumadeen took 2-70, the other two 0-150 between them as India made 406-4 and squared the series. In the changing room afterwards, Lloyd was coldly scathing: 'Gentlemen, how many runs do you need to bowl a team out?'

Imtiaz Ali played in just that one Test, and although the other two spinners appeared in the next, they bowled only 13 overs in all. India had reaped the whirlwind. Lloyd, now certain that his instincts about pace and spin were right, unleashed four fast bowlers on them, setting Michael Holding to bowl round the wicket. Result: mayhem, and a win by 10 wickets.

At the end of the first day, India were 178-1. On the second, three of their batsmen were in hospital: tiny Gundappa Viswanath's middle finger broken by a bouncer, Anshuman Gaekwad hit on the temple, Brijesh Patel in the mouth.

Bishen Bedi protested to the umpires, but Ralph Gosein maintained that a ridge had suddenly appeared on the pitch (!), whereupon Bedi declared the second innings closed with only five wickets down as a protest against intimidatory bowling, giving the West Indies the series 2-1.

The rest is history that's still going on. The all-conquering all-out pace attack, beginning with a 3-0 win in England a few months later, was here to stay. That 406-4 is still the record, but the other Test-playing countries haven't thanked India for it.

During Australia's first innings of the first Test, in November 1985, New Zealand all-rounder Richard Hadlee moved under a catch offered by Geoff Lawson from a ball by spinner Vaughan Brown, and held it to make Australia 179-9.

Great for the Kiwis, who won by an innings on the way to taking a series in Australia for the first time, and for Brown (it was the only Test wicket he ever took).

Not so good for Hadlee himself. He'd picked up the first eight wickets to fall, and finished with 9-52. His catch cost him the chance of equalling Jim Laker's record of all ten wickets in a Test innings.

A birdie 3 on the 72nd hole at the 1989 British Open earned Mark Calcavecchia of the States a place in a play-off for the title against two Australians: Wayne Grady, who'd led Calcavecchia by three strokes after the third round, and Greg Norman, the 1986 champion, who'd birdied the first six holes of the last round on the way to a typically barnstorming 64.

This broke the course record, and the barn seemed to be well and truly stormed when Norman birdied the first of the four holes used in the play-off. He birdied the next as well, but Calcavecchia clung on to the Shark's tail by doing the same, then drew level

by parring the third, which both Australians bogeyed.

The last play-off hole was the 18th, which held that recent good memory for the American. There was soon an even better one: his second shot, a superb five-iron from 202 yards, took him to within five feet of the hole. Grady wasn't in contention.

As for Norman, not for the first time he found a singular way of losing a Major. Lashing into his tee shot with a power the other two simply didn't have, he found a bunker which had appeared to be beyond reach. Too strong for his own good, he had to go for broke with his second, but hit the top of the sand.

After Grady missed his attempt at a birdie, Calcavecchia had three putts for the Open. He used only one, made up for the disappointment of losing the previous year's Masters by one stroke to Sandy Lyle, and hasn't won another Major. Grady won *his* only one, the USPGA, the following year, Norman his second – only his second – in 1993.

At the 1991 world swimming championships, Melvin Stewart of the USA beat the fading giant Michael Gross to win the 200m butterfly title – and deprive himself of a probable $200 000.

This was the prize offered by sponsors for a world record set in the States. The final had been in Perth, Western Australia – and Stewart's record was an outstanding one, breaking Gross' already formidable mark by more than half a second. His chances of undercutting his new time, without the adrenalin of a world final, weren't great. In fact the record still stands. 'If I'd known I was going so fast, I'd have slowed down.'

When Amanda Guild was named tenpin bowler of the week by Michigan's *Saginaw News* in 1991, her picture appeared in the paper, where it was recognised as that of a woman who'd fled Tennessee to escape drug charges. She was arrested just before her next league match.

Left, facing page: *Greg Norman about to cut his own throat at Troon*
(Popperfoto)

THE IMPORTANT THING IS NOT THE WINNING BUT THE TAKING PART

Henry Taylor won five England caps at rugby union, Charles Montague Sawyer two. They would have won one more each if the 1881 game in Scotland hadn't been postponed twice.

By the time it was played, Sawyer was unavailable – but Taylor arrived at the wrong railway station and the team left the right one without him. His absence let in Frank Wright (a student at the Edinburgh Academy) for his only cap, while Sawyer was replaced at half-back by Campbell Rowley, a forward. A muddled England team was held to a draw by Scotland, who'd lost the previous year's match 29-7 in today's money.

The main casualty of the postponements was one JE Junor, who was picked to play but had to leave for India before the game eventually took place, and never won an England cap.

THE RUSSIANS AREN'T COMING. The Tsarist shooting team that arrived at the 1908 Olympics in London discovered that all the events had been completed several days earlier. They were still using the Julian calendar while most other countries had adopted the Gregorian.

The 1896 US athletics team did the same thing in reverse, arriving twelve days early according to their Gregorian calendar, but only one day according to the Julian, which the Greeks were using. That single day was enough to keep the Americans off this list: they dominated the track and field at those first modern Olympics, winning 9 of the 12 gold medals.

In 1928, track athlete Emerson 'Bud' Spencer set a 400 metre world record of 47.0 that wasn't beaten for four years, but a remarkable howler in the US Olympic trials put paid to his chances of the Olympic title.

Finishing only fast enough to qualify for the next round, he suddenly realised there was no next round: he'd been running in the final.

He qualified for the relay team, which won the gold medal in Amsterdam, breaking the world record by nearly two seconds.

Thomas Fahrner's similar mistake in the Olympic pool also cost him a probable gold. In 1984, when the Soviet boycott deprived the 400m freestyle of Vladimir Salnikov, the West German became one of the favourites.

But, like a novice (he wasn't), he tried to conserve energy by swimming his preliminary race just fast enough to qualify for the final – and managed only the ninth fastest time, one short of a place. He swam 3:50.91 in the consolation final, breaking the Olympic record set by George DiCarlo in the final proper.

Fahrner won a silver medal with West Germany's team in the 4x400 freestyle relay, and a bronze in the same event four years later, but never a gold.

Four Turkish freestyle wrestlers who'd won gold medals at the 1948 Olympics – Nasuh Akar, Celal Atik, Gazanfer Bilge and Yasar Dogu – were favourites to repeat the feat in 1952, but couldn't take part because their federation forgot to post their entries.

On the track, or rather off it, the Romanian women's 800m team missed the 1988 Olympics for the same reason. Again an almost certain medal went begging, possibly the gold: from 1984 to 1993, Doina Melinte and Ella Kovacs won six titles between them in the Olympics, European Cup and European Indoors.

Torben Ulrich, the oldest Davis Cup player ever (48 in 1976), and one of the great eccentrics of tennis (he lost his national title when he walked off court to go and watch the 1966 World Cup final!), was disqualified (and suspended by his own Copenhagen club) when he wandered in late for a doubles match at Wimbledon in 1954.

Spanish Steps, a horse who might well have beaten L'Escargot in

Foot in mouth
"I make no apologies for their absence but I'm sorry they're not here."
MURRAY WALKER

Foot in mouth

"England have their noses in front, not only actually but metaphorically too."
TONY COZIER

the 1971 Cheltenham Gold Cup, didn't run in it: the wife of trainer Ted Courage entered the name of another horse (Trajan) with Weatherby's, who didn't spot the mistake.

After Miruts Yifter had finished third in the 1972 Olympic 10 000m, he was expected to give Lasse Viren another battle in the 5000 final. He didn't even make it to the track for the start of his heat.

There are various theories. That he spent too long in the toilet. That he got out of the toilet in time but couldn't find his way through the stadium. That he found his way through the stadium but was directed to the wrong check-in by one of the guards.

Whichever, he was kept out of the 1976 Games by the African boycott (Viren retained both titles) but won the 5000/10 000 double in 1980.

In 1988, bantamweight boxer Eduard Paululum, who was set to become the first competitor from the Pacific island of Vanuatu to take part in the Olympics, consumed a heavyweight breakfast before his first weigh-in, and had be disqualified for being overweight (by a single pound).

Stephen Roche, Tour de France winner in 1987, was eliminated from the 1991 race on only the second day after arriving seven minutes late for the start of a time trial. As in the Yifter case, there was talk of toilet trouble.

Lars Hall was another one keen to get involved (or rather not). He arrived 20 minutes late during the 1952 Olympic modern pentathlon and would have been disqualified from the whole event if the shooting hadn't been running late (the USSR were protesting a decision). Reprieved, Hall went on to win the Olympic title, which he retained in 1956.

NOT SO FAST EDDIE

Hart and Robinson 1972

Wim Essajas was a one-off. In every sense. The first competitor ever entered for the Olympics by Surinam, he travelled alone to the Rome Games of 1960 and would have arrived at the track for the afternoon heats of the 800 metres in plenty of time except for one thing. They'd been held in the morning. So Wim Essajas went back to Surinam, who didn't send another competitor to the Games till 1968.

All very tragi-comic, but what's he doing on this page? Um, to make the point that while this kind of thing can befall a man on his own in a foreign country, with no advisors or back-up, it couldn't happen to the United States, with their hundreds of athletes and army of officials. They wouldn't lose a single competitor like that. No, sir. They lost two of them.

Eddie Hart and Rey Robinson arrived at the 1972 Munich Olympics as co-holders of the world record over 100 metres. It was something of a specious honour: their hand-timed mark of 9.9 was probably two yards slower than Jim Hines' electronic world record of 9.95. Oh, and Robinson had set his 'record' while finishing second to Hart, so his claim wouldn't be taken seriously nowadays. Still, at the time, they could lay some sort of claim to being regarded as the world's fastest humans.

They went some way to living up to that billing in the first round in Munich, winning their races at a stroll. Back at the Olympic village, they ambled down to the bus stop on their way back to the stadium for the second round heats, which were due to start at 7.00 in the evening. It was now just after 4.00.

While waiting for the bus, Robinson went across to the headquarters of ABC Television and stood idly watching some runners lining up for a sprint race. A re-run of the morning's heats? Nope, he was told: this was live TV. A horrified Robinson realised he was watching the very race he should have been competing in.

He and Hart and the third American sprinter Robert Taylor were rushed to the stadium in an

ABC car, but it was too late for the two record holders. Robinson was due to run in Heat 1, Hart in 2, but they didn't arrive until the start of the third, just enough time for Taylor to make some hasty preparations and get to his blocks.

In the circumstances, he did well to finish second behind Valery Borzov of the USSR, the real Fastest Man In The World at the time, who ran his best ever electronic time of 10.07 ahead of Taylor's strong 10.16.

In the final, Taylor again finished second to Borzov (who won as he liked, hands in the air long before the finish) then joined forces with Hart to help win the relay - but Robinson never won an Olympic medal.

Reasons? They used to vary. At first it was rumoured that coach Stan Wright had read the 15.00 start as 5 o'clock instead of 3. Then it was said, and it's now generally believed, that he'd been reading from a schedule that was eighteen months out of date. Either way, Wright was one of the great wrongs. Wim Essajas would definitely have approved.

Above: I have seen the future of sprinting, and it's not me. After winning his heat, Eddie Hart looks ahead to the second round (Popperfoto)

PICK OF THE WEAK

and other selectorial gaffes

By 1953 Cliff Morgan was already the most brilliant fly-half in Wales. The selectors, however, got it into their heads that he couldn't function without Rex Willis at scrum-half. When injury kept the latter out of the opening match of the Five Nations championship, Morgan was replaced by a skilful new cap Roy Burnett, whose club partner Billy Williams was picked at scrum-half: a move which cost Wales the title. England won at the Arms Park and neither of the Newport half-backs was ever capped again. Morgan was back for the three remaining matches (with and without Willis), all of which Wales won – but England took the championship by a single point.

Although he was only 15 in 1979, Jahangir Khan was already good enough to win the world amateur squash title, beating Britain's Phil Kenyon in the final. The decision to leave him out of the final of the team event handed the gold medal to Britain, who won 2-1.

Players who came back with a vengeance

Basil Maclear, a fast bodyswerving winger, was turned down by the England rugby selectors for being too individualistic (the kind of individual who wore white gloves on the pitch). Born in Hampshire, he played for Cork County and was picked 11 times for Ireland, making his debut in 1905 on his home club ground – against England. He scored a try, made two others and kicked a conversion in the 17-3 win then repeated the dose the following year (try and conversion) as Ireland won 16-6. He was on the winning side in all three of his matches against England, and scored four tries (including a brilliant one against the Springboks) and three conversions in internationals.

Foot in mouth
"Those are the sort of doors that get opened if you don't close them."
TERRY VENABLES

In 1954 Norman Read moved from England to New Zealand before writing to the AAA asking to be given a trial for the British athletics team. Thanks but no thanks.

Turned down by New Zealand too, he did well enough in local races to eventually be chosen for the 50 km walk at the 1956 Olympics in Melbourne, where he survived a late rush to the starting line and overcame fierce heat and the European champion Yevgeny Maskinskov to finish more than half an hour ahead of the first British walker (Albert Johnson in 8th place) and take a surprise gold medal.

[Three years later, Read made a prize blunder of his own. The story goes that he was lying a close second in the New Zealand long-distance championship race when he noticed the leader Kevin Keogh pick up the pace with still a fair way to go to the finish. Read held back to conserve his strength – only to discover that Keogh had noticed a railway line just ahead, with a goods train approaching on it. He nipped across, leaving the Olympic champion to do more conserving than he wanted while the freight wagons rumbled past: 1,289 of them.]

Cambridge made a late change in their team for the 1842 Boat Race, bringing in AB (Arthur Becher) Pollock as cox – even though he hadn't sat in front of an eight (or steered any kind of boat on the Thames) for more than a year. Not surprisingly, the Light Blues wandered all over the river, losing to Oxford by 13 seconds. It was said that Pollock 'steered badly but redeemed himself by cheering well'.

Although he broke his own 440 yards world record by a full second (46.0), track athlete Ben Eastman was better over 800 metres. He would have been heavy favourite to win at the longer distance, but his coach entered him for only the 400 in the 1932 Olympics.

Fair enough, you might think. That world record was yards ahead of anyone else. But he'd recently lost twice to the up-and-coming Bill Carr, who was already looking like one of the greatest quarter-milers of all time. Eastman knew it too: Carr was too strong for him in the home stretch, and his own chances were much better at the longer distance.

Unfortunately for Eastman, Carr's trainer (Lawson Robertson) had been chosen ahead of his own (Dink Templeton) as coach to the US Olympic team, and as a result Templeton had something to prove.

Eastman did his best. In the final, he equalled his old world record – but Carr broke it ahead of him, coming from behind again to set an Olympic record that lasted twenty years. Bill beat

Peter Taylor, Brian Clough's right hand man at Derby and Forest, was one of the very best judges of a footballer. Well, usually.

He made his biggest mistake, he thought, on a drab August evening in Southend. The player he'd gone to watch had a bad night, making his runs at the wrong time or not making them at all, contributing to Scunthorpe's 3-0 defeat. Though the asking price was only £15 000, Taylor wrote him off as being too small.

Two years later in 1971, the same tich was playing just behind two bigger front men (Taylor admitted he should have known this would turn out to be his best position), timing his runs rather better and costing Liverpool £30 000. Joseph Kevin Keegan had arrived.

Foot in mouth

"He is without doubt the greatest sweeper in the world. I'd say. At a guess."
RON ATKINSON

Ben by two yards and won another gold in the relay. Two years later, running in his best event, Eastman equalled the 800 metres world record, but he never won an Olympic title.

In the first two months of their 1974 tour, the British Lions had ridden roughshod over their South African opponents, winning all 17 matches including two against the Springboks, the second by 28-9 (worth 38-9 today).

South Africa had fielded six new caps in the first Test, six more in the second (seven changes in all), and now picked yet another six for the third (an astonishing ten changes from the second match). A tale of entire teams, then – but the selection of one player in particular showed which part of the barrel was being scraped.

When the scrum-halves who played in the first two Tests – Roy McCallum and Paul Bayvel – both reported injured, the Springbok selectors called for some fiddlers three – Gert Schutte, Barry Wolmarans and Gerrie Sonnekus – even though it was clear they knew precious little about the passing ability of any of them. In the end they plumped for Sonnekus, who didn't show any at all. Plump was the operative word: until a few weeks earlier, he'd been a No. 8!

South Africa, playing their third completely different pair of half-backs in as many Tests, lost 26-9 to a Lions team that missed any number of try-scoring opportunities. All gone: match, series, Afrikaaner self-respect.

Sonnekus, who'd shovelled all kinds of terrifying passes in the general direction of his fly-half, was left out of international rugby for ten seasons. When he returned, he contributed to the two biggest defeats England had ever suffered: 33-15 and 35-9. He scored a try in the second Test – playing at No. 8.

Selectors who had one too many

Joe Smith was one of football's personalities in the Twenties, his ferocious shooting earning five England caps and helping Bolton win the FA Cup in 1923 (as captain) and 1926. Although he was 37 by the time he moved to Stockport in Division 3 North, a record crowd came to see his first match, against Stoke in March 1927.

County drew 2-2, a good result against a good team – but they'd overlooked one detail: Joe Smith wasn't eligible. Before the game, Stockport chairman Ernest Barlow had been handed a telegram telling him that Smith's registration hadn't been confirmed. Barlow decided to keep the matter to himself.

County were fined £100, had two points deducted, and were allowed to field Smith only in matches sanctioned by a League committee. All of which helped cost them promotion, which they didn't achieve for another ten years. Stoke went up instead.

In September 1992, playing their first European Cup tie since the 1975 final, Leeds United went to Stuttgart, where they defended comfortably for an hour before over-confidence set in. The dangerous Fritz Walter scored twice in six minutes, Leeds lost 3-0, played infinitely better to win 4-1 at home, but were knocked out by Andreas Buck's away goal.

However . . . before the return at Elland Road, team manager Christoph Daum and general manager Dieter Hoeness had given the referee a team sheet with 16 names, including four foreign players: Slobodan Dubajic and Jovica Simanic from the old Yugoslavia, Eyjolfur Sverrisson of Iceland, and Swiss midfielder Adrian Knup. Mistake No. 1. The allowance was five foreigners per team per match – but only three who hadn't lived in the country for five years.

This wouldn't have been fatal if the official observer had done his job. A fortnight earlier, UEFA's man at the match had noticed an extra foreigner in the Cup-Winners' Cup tie between Hanover and Werder Bremen, and issued a warning. Here, Edgar Obertufer overlooked things. Mistake No. 2.

Finally, mistake No. 3: Stuttgart fielded all four imports during the match. The English press generally missed the significance, a German journalist didn't, the rules demanded that Leeds be awarded the tie

This, though, was too much of a nettle for UEFA's grasp. They found a convenient solution by awarding the match to Leeds 3-0, levelling the aggregate score at 3-3 to set up a play-off which Stuttgart lost 2-1 to substitute Carl Shutt's late goal. The fair result.

There had been no question of the Germans trying to slip players through the net; it was a simple blunder. And an expensive one. With the likes of Walter, Knup, Immel and Buchwald in the squad, there was every chance of reaching the lucrative mini-league stage, possibly the final itself. Even just the two legs of the second round against Rangers would have brought in the *geld*. Stuttgart official Ulrich Ruf was just one of many who agreed that Daum's oversight had cost the club millions.

In 1965, the year that the US Amateur golf championship switched to matchplay, Bob Dickson led at the 70th hole but lost to Robert

Murphy by a single stroke – after being handed a massive four-shot penalty for having one club too many in his bag, even though he'd carried it for only the first two holes of the second round, it wasn't his club in the first place, and he didn't use it!

Unpicking the team

The Arsenal that Herbert Chapman built dominated the 1930s, winning five League championships and two FA Cups, providing a record seven players for a single England team. In 1932–33 they scored more goals than any other club in the country (118) in winning the first of three consecutive Division I titles. On January 14th they appeared at Fellows Park in the third round of the Cup.

While Chapman was spending record sums to build his squads, the town of Walsall was suffering the worst of the Depression. A 'Spending for Employment' campaign was set up: whatever you can spare – to have a coat mended, say, a door repaired, anything – spend it to provide local people with work. Only 11,149 could afford to watch the Arsenal match.

Walsall the team hadn't won away all season. Although unbeaten at home, they lay 54 places below Arsenal in the League, 10th in Division 3 North – and Chapman decided it was safe enough to do a little experimenting.

Out went a string of first choices: Bob John, Eddie Hapgood, Joe Hulme, Jack Lambert. In came Norman Sidey and Tommy Black in defence, Billy Warnes and Charlie Walsh up front. Of the four, only Sidey had any first-team experience – but Walsh, at least, wasn't lacking in confidence: he thought himself the best centre-forward at the club. He spread the word that he was about to play the game of his life.

He did. He missed at least four clear-cut chances, including a perfect cross from Cliff Bastin that hit him on the shoulder, and a pass that was on its way to the unmarked David Jack before he got in the way. After a goalless first half, Chapman moved him aside and put Jack at centre-forward, but the tide was already moving one way.

Walsall, on a win bonus of £5 a man (average wage £6), had sailed into Arsenal from the start, cutting Herbie Roberts' eye, fouling Bastin and Alex James. On the hour, Fred Lee's cross was headed in by Gilbert Alsop, who was then fouled in the penalty area by Black (another new boy having a bad one). Bill Sheppard's penalty sealed one of biggest cup upsets imaginable.

Arsenal's seven internationals (Bastin, James and Jack were among the best of all time) lived to play another day. So too did Sidey (just). But Black was transferred to Plymouth within a week, Walsh to Brentford within a month, Warnes to Norwich at the end of the season.

The real blame, though, fell on Chapman and his assistant Tom

Whittaker: 'We made a blunder today, Tom, but nobody is going to know.' Sorry, Herbert, couldn't resist it.

Between the wars, American sprinting and quarter-miling was so strong that their relay quartets won Olympic titles without having to call up some of the individual medallists: Charlie Paddock and Jackson Scholz in 1924, Eddie Tolan, Ralph Metcalfe and Ben Eastman in 1932, etc.

In 1936, however, coach Lawson Robertson took no chances with the short relay, drafting in Metcalfe and Jesse Owens to make certain of the gold medal and world record. But Robertson made a mistake in not paying the same attention to the 4x400.

The fact is that the sprinters would almost certainly have won even without Owens and Metcalfe, but the 400m men faced a real threat from the British: Godfrey Brown had missed the individual gold by only 0.02 seconds, with Bill Roberts just 0.03 away from the bronze, while Godfrey Rampling had won a relay silver four years earlier. The US needed all hands to the pump.

Instead, Robertson left out the Olympic champion and world record holder Archie Williams, bronze medallist Jim LuValle, and Glenn Hardin, the Ed Moses of his day, Olympic champion over the hurdles, who later set a world record that lasted 19 years. The chosen four – Harold Cagle, Bob Young, Ed O'Brien, Alf Fitch – finished second, 12 yards behind the British.

Backing the wrong horse – or rider

Northern Dancer sired an entire dynasty of top-class thorough-breds, including the mighty Nijinsky (1970 Triple Crown winner) and The Minstrel (winner of the 1977 Derby). Sometimes, however, he didn't quite do the big business . . .

Snaafi Dancer was a Northern Dancer colt who had Sheikh Mohamed and Robert Sangster at each other's throats during the 1983 Kentucky yearling sales. The Sheikh eventually got him for $10.2 million, at the time easily the world record for a yearling – and the biggest waste of money in bloodstock history. Hopeless in training, Snaafi Dancer was never allowed anywhere near a racecourse.

But then perhaps this was an animal with a sense of humour (with a name like that, he'd have to have been), or a taste for revenge on the whole overblown business. Even at stud, he didn't give his all: only two of the mares in his first season produced foals.

Foot in mouth
"I wonder whether Man United are missing the absence of Bruce."
TREVOR FRANCIS

Two years later, Sangster's syndicate got their horse. At £13.1 million, Seattle Dancer broke cousin Snaafi's record – and was almost as much of a disappointment, winning just a couple of Group 2 races in Ireland.

Below: During yet another win for Dessie, Simon Sherwood has time to compose a thank-you note for Colin Brown (Popperfoto)

In the King George VI Rank Chase at Kempton Park in 1986, Colin Brown chose to ride Combs Ditch in preference to another David Elsworth horse, a 16-1 shot who carried Simon Sherwood to

victory ahead of a quality field (Wayward Lad, Forgive 'N Forget, Combs Ditch himself). The white horse was here to stay.

Colin Brown wasn't. Sherwood rode Desert Orchid to win the 1988 Whitbread Gold Cup and the 1989 Cheltenham Gold Cup.

The battle for the 1987 flat jockeys' championship was one of the tightest ever. At Doncaster on the very last day, trailing Steve Cauthen by three with three races left, Pat Eddery began by winning the Armistice Stakes on Night Pass, after which trainer Ray Laing offered him the ride on Sharp Reminder in the EBF Remembrance Stakes. Eddery chose Vilusi instead. He finished fourth, Sharp Reminder won the race, Cauthen the title.

Everyone knows Lester Piggott's record in the Derby (nine wins, three more than any other jockey) and the way he achieved some of it: displacing the riders of fancied horses at the last minute, as when he 'jocked off' Bill Williamson on Roberto in 1972. Sometimes he didn't get the ride he wanted, but it didn't always matter . . .

In 1977 he had his eye on the 9-4 favourite Blushing Groom, and approached the Aga Khan, who turned him down and kept faith with Henri Samani, who had no experience of Epsom, the most difficult course in the world on which to ride in a big field.

Samani did his best, but he was no Piggott. Lester, on The Minstrel, outmanoeuvred him at the top of the hill and won by a head from Hot Grove with Blushing Groom, watched by a blushing Aga, five lengths behind. Piggott won the eighth of his nine Derbies, Samani never won it at all.

Occasionally, though, owners should have resisted the temptation.

The star of Ryan Price's stable in 1975 was the chunky little grey colt Bruni, whom he intended to hold back for the St Leger. However, owner Charles St George was keen to run him in the Derby – and to replace stable jockey Tony Murray with Piggott.

Price argued against both decisions. He thought Murray knew the horse better and anyway didn't regard Bruni as mature enough to handle a rough-house like the Derby, especially on firm ground.

But St George got his way – and some just desserts. Piggott kept

Foot in mouth

"Northern trainers have got a lot of ammunition in their larder."
RICHARD PITMAN

Bruni on a very short rein, which he didn't like, and couldn't stop him being bounced sideways at Tattenham Corner. Bruni finished 14th, with very sore shins, and soon caught a virus which he transferred to the rest of the stable, so that Price saddled only 25 winners in three months.

Bruni didn't return to the track for the same length of time – then, with Murray back on board, won the St Leger by an astonishing 10 lengths ahead of Piggott on King Pellinore.

That should have been that. Price, proved right, wanted to retire the horse for the season, knowing that he'd shot his bolt. But St George, a slow learner, insisted on running Bruni in the Arc de Triomphe, where he finished seventh, going backwards at the end.

The following year, St George did it again, pairing the unfortunate animal with Piggott in the King George & Queen Elizabeth Stakes. The chemistry hadn't changed. Lester, in Price's opinion, rode indecisively, on a horse he clearly had no confidence in. Last at Swinley Bottom, he tried to make up ground on the inside, always a gamble, and finished second in a race he could have won. In the Arc, much the same story as the previous season, fading to fifth.

By the time Price was allowed to do what he'd always intended, train him for the later cup races, the zip had gone. Bruni was disqualified in one race, finished fourth and second, then broke down in another. He didn't run again, and hadn't added anything to his stud value. That sequence of decisions had cost St George a packet.

Last but not at all, the ultimate cock-up in selection

In 1906 the first South African rugby touring team arrived at the old Crystal Palace to be confronted by an England team which included the one and only Arnold Alcock, a doctor from Guy's Hospital and a persevering but unexceptional forward whose selection was a complete mystery to everyone, not least Alcock himself. He seems to have coped well enough (no match reports singled him out for criticism) but won only this one cap.

Hardly surprising, given that he was the only misprint ever to play for England, capped by mistake in place of Lancelot Slocock, a well-known player who scored three tries in his eight internationals.

SPINWASHED

England (minus Gower) in India 1992–93

When David Gower was left out of England's tour to the West Indies in 1990 despite his century against Australia at Lord's and his bravery in two previous Caribbean series, no-one was altogether surprised. This time Cap'n Gooch was determined to surround himself with fellow disciples of the great god Sweat. No room for anyone who gave the impression of actually enjoying a tour.

So Gower didn't go, and Botham didn't go, and it nearly worked. After 30 Tests spread over 16 years, England won one against the West Indies, and were very unlucky not to take the series. When they shared the next one against the same opposition without giving Gower a game (he'd been fined a thousand quid for his Tiger Moth exploits in Australia), there seemed to be no way back for Lulu.

But then the waters began to muddy. Recalled for the last three Tests against Pakistan in 1992, Gower averaged exactly 50, passed

Boycott's England record total of runs, and seemed to have booked his tour place, especially as he'd generally done well against India: winning a series there as captain, scoring a double century at Edgbaston,.

Instead: shock omission. Official excuse: too old. This when England were recalling Mike Gatting (35, the same age as Gower) and John Emburey (40) to play under Gooch (39). MCC members called a sack-the-selectors meeting, Gower issued thanks-for-your-support-but-let's-get-on-with-the-tour statements, there were dark mutterings in the Commons.

Worse still, this was a squad picked with half a eye on the one-day matches – so no place for Jack Russell behind the stumps, England deciding that two batsmen who put on big

Below: How many ways can you say 'I told you so'? DI Gower's first test as a reporter in India
(Allsport/Ben Radford)

pads, Alec Stewart and Richard Blakey, could keep wicket on pitches they weren't used to. They couldn't. Stewart gave up the job after the first Test, and Blakey (winning his first two caps) didn't look the part at all. Picked for his batting, he scored a grand total of 6 runs in the Tests at an average of 1.75.

Some of the bowling didn't look any better in

Above: The pigeon comes home to roost. Gooch out for 17 in the first Test
(Allsport/Chris Cole)

prospect: a surprise recall for eternal under-achiever Paul Jarvis, a first tour for left-arm seamer Paul Taylor. Both played in the opening Test in Calcutta, where Emburey and Phil Tufnell were kept out of an attack that included four seamers and left the spinning in the hands of a very green leg-spinner (Ian Salisbury) and a part-timer (Graeme Hick). Sunil Gavaskar wasn't impressed: 'Tufnell, to my mind, is the best left-arm spinner in the world, and not to have included him was a blunder of monumental proportions.' Ah yes, the kind of quote that's music to the ears of this writer.

Salisbury took 1-88, a clearly nervous Taylor 1-74 in his only Test so far, England lost by 8 wickets and each of the next two Tests by an innings. After a whitewash by Australia and two blackwashes by the West Indies, this was the first time they'd lost all three on the subcontinent. They also lost five of the 8 one-dayers and to Sri Lanka for the first time. Gower, commentating for BSkyB, didn't know whether to laugh or cry (oh yes he did), especially as Gooch averaged only 11.75 in the Tests and came home early.

While the tour fell about their ears, the players had generally hung in there – and there were some genuine plusses: Neil Fairbrother, the persevering Jarvis, first Test centuries for Hick and Chris Lewis, a first abroad for Robin Smith – but the selection had handicapped them from the start.

Head of selectors Ted Dexter reacted decisively, telling the players to shave and get their hair cut, so it really must have been serious (he resigned in August) – while manager Keith Fletcher admitted that 'our selection policy has misfired. My feeling is that we have to pick our best possible squad to win Test matches.' Oh well, so at least a lesson had been learned.

No no, just kidding. The very next summer (still no Gower, still no Russell) England didn't pick left-handers to counter Shane Warne till it was too late, lost the first two Tests (making it seven in a row) and the Ashes series 4-1. Oh, and Gooch (no longer captain) went past Gower's England record number of runs in Tests. Enough to make Lulu wanna shout.

ONE-CAP WONDER BLUNDERS

With the 1875 soccer international against Scotland about to start, England were still a man short. WH (William Henry) Carr of the Owlerton club in Sheffield had missed his train down to London, and the Scottish captain Joe Taylor offered to postpone the kick-off. Gosh no, said Charles Alcock, awfully nobly: we'll start with just ten of the chaps. He put one of his many forwards in goal – AG (Alexander George) Bonsor of the Wanderers – and settled down to hold out.

After a quarter of an hour, an apologetic Carr hurried onto the pitch, went in goal, let in both goals in a 2-2 draw, and didn't play for England again. Nor did Alcock, who put the hosts 2-1 ahead, or Bonsor, or five other players.

Having a Test match named after you for doing something right is standard stuff (Laker 1956, Massie 1972, Botham 1981, etc). To put your moniker on one for the opposite reason takes a special kind of performance, the kind that makes Frederick William Tate a hero in anyone's book, especially this one.

Tate's Match was the fourth of the 1902 series, at Old Trafford. In Australia's first innings, he took 0-44 and missed a famous catch off the Australian captain Joe Darling who went on to make a critical 51. In their second innings, Fred and his slow-medium off-spinners made some amends by taking two wickets for only seven runs (and holding a catch) to help shoot them out for 86. That might have redeemed him if England hadn't then collapsed to 116-9. The last man in was FW Tate. A natural No.11, he'd nevertheless made a redoubtable 5 not out in the first innings and England now needed only 8 to win.

Before he could bat, a heavy shower added to the tension by driving the players off the field. When they came back, he hit the first ball he received from Jack Saunders for four, but was clean bowled in the same over. Australia won by 3 runs and took the series 2-1. Fred Tate played in only this one Test. His son Maurice was England's best bowler in the 1920s.

For their first match of the 1914 Five Nations championship, England and Wales fielded 11 new caps between them, and provided one of Twickenham's great cliffhanging internationals, Welsh pack against English backs. At half-time England led 5-4, a prelude to the Willie Watts show.

In 1881, JP (John Purvis) Hawtrey was brought into the England team after some 'great goalkeeping' for the Old Etonians. Scotland, a month later, were a different proposition. They won 6-1, still England's record home defeat, and the 'feeble and uncertain' Hawtrey fumbled Joe Lindsay's shot to let in David Hill for the important second goal, generally 'failed miserably', and won only this single cap.

At first, he had Ronnie Poulton as his assistant. Poulton (later Poulton-Palmer) was the dashing hero of English rugby, much mourned when shot by a sniper in the First World War, a sidestepping centre whose try and near-miss against the 1913 Springboks is the stuff of legend. Here he looked infinitely more mortal, letting his opposite number Watts in for the only Welsh try of the match. England trailed 9-5 with eight minutes left.

Watts, winning his first cap, then repaid the compliment with interest. Covering on his own goal line, he took his eye off the ball and let it slip straight to Charles 'Cherry' Pillman, the famous, idiosyncratic English No. 8, who went over for the try. FE (Frederick Ernest) Chapman's second conversion won the match 10-9 for England, who went on to win their second successive Grand Slam. But for Watts' fumble, Wales would have won the Slam themselves. He wasn't capped again.

In their first match of the 1957 championship, Wales and England fought out an undistinguished match dominated by the forwards (the Welsh back row gave the new England fly-half Ricky Bartlett a tough time).

The game was decided by a single score. The England flanker Alan 'Ned' Ashcroft broke clear along the left touchline to within 10 yards of the Welsh line. From the lineout, the Neath winger Keith Maddocks took a step offside.

Even though he was nowhere near the action, a penalty was given – in front of the posts. Full-back Dennis Allison couldn't miss, England went on to win the Grand Slam, Maddocks won only this one cap.

When Barry John, partnering Gareth Edwards for the first time in an international, took the scrum-half's pass to drop a goal, Wales were only 5 points behind New Zealand at the Arms Park in 1967. Against Fred Allen's brilliant team (Tremain, Meads, Laidlaw, McCormick), this was no small feat. With minutes left, Wales were knocking on the door.

Thirteen minutes later they brought it down on top of themselves. The All Blacks, awarded a penalty on the Welsh 10-yard line, called up McCormick, whose kick at goal into the wind fell only just short. The Welsh No. 8, new cap John Jeffery of Newport, picked the ball up and, under pressure from Bill Davis, threw a horrible pass back over his shoulder. The rest of the team, taken by surprise, missed it, Davis dived in to score by the posts. Wales lost 13-6, haven't beaten New Zealand since 1953, and Jeffery didn't win another etc etc.

Foot in mouth
"I won't say it's easier, but it's easier."
RAY ILLINGWORTH

In 1973 England arrived in Auckland for the international against the All Blacks as the most sacrificial of lambs, already slaughtered by the three provincial sides they'd played on tour, now facing the likes of Going, Kirkpatrick, Batty and Bryan Williams (and former All Black winger Frank McMullen as referee).

In the event, the wolves came out from under the sheepskin coats: little Jan Webster had a big game at scrum-half, and a very good England pack outplayed the All Black forwards, scoring two tries in the second half, both presented to them by the nervousness of one man.

In place of short, stocky, steady Joe Karam, New Zealand had brought in Bob Lendrum at full-back. In the first half, he missed the conversion of Batty's opening try. In the second, with the All Blacks leading 10-6, he missed touch from his own 25, setting up Webster, who ran the ball back before feeding his forwards: prop Brian 'Stack' Stevens crossed for the equalising try.

Five minutes from time, Lendrum positioned himself under a high kick, caught it, then let it drop. Again the ubiquitous Webster was first to the ball, this time to feed Alan Old, who found Tony Neary for the winning try. It was the only time New Zealand have been beaten at home by one of the British countries. Karam was back for the next five matches and Lendrum didn't win another cap.

In 1978, after losing bravely in Paris, England played the exceptional Welsh team on a Twickenham mudheap, a match decided by penalty goals. Alastair Hignell missed with four out of six. With only eight minutes left, Phil Bennett had also scored twice (from three attempts). Then the Welsh forwards marched to the edge of the England 22, and Bob Mordell, a curly-haired Rosslyn Park flanker brought in to replace the injured Peter Dixon, handled in the ruck.

Bennett kicked his third penalty goal to win the match 9-6, Wales went on to the Grand Slam, England (with the world class Dixon back on the flank) won their two remaining matches in the championship, and Mordell went to play rugby league with Oldham and Kent Invicta before rejoining Rosslyn Park after reinstatement in 1990, by which time he was 39. Typical generosity by the Rugby Union.

England's footballers arrived in Rome at the end of a highly successful 1960-61 season (unbeaten, 41 goals in seven matches) to play a friendly against an inexperienced Italian team. Two goals late in the first half left the teams level until the last quarter of an hour.

Before that, one captain (goalkeeper Renzo Buffon) had broken his nose on the knee of the other (Johnny Haynes) and had to go off, to be replaced by Giuseppe Vavassori of Juventus.

Eighteen minutes later, Sergio Brighenti (who'd scored in the 2-2 draw at Wembley two years earlier) put Italy 2-1 ahead – but England were level within three minutes (Hitchens again) and won the match five minutes from time (Greaves). Vavassori, who'd let in one of the goals between his legs, didn't play for Italy again: an international career of 34 minutes.

CAPTAIN, THE SHIP IS SINKING

failures of leadership

The Wanderers, a team made up of players from a variety of clubs, won the first FA Cup and were favourites to keep it in 1873.

Oxford University pushed them hard in the final, dominating the first twenty minutes with youthful pace and good teamwork. Before long, however, the combined team's experience (they fielded seven internationals to the University's four) and aggressive dribbling began to tell, and they went ahead on the half-hour when their captain Arthur Kinnaird, the red-bearded Perthshire landowner, ran past both full-backs to score from close in.

After that: attrition. Much collegiate pressing, whiskered men holding the fort. Towards the end, the Oxford captain, the England international Arnold Kirke Smith, made the decision to reinforce his attack by moving AJ (Andrew John) Leach upfield and therefore playing without a goalkeeper. Gasp. The press talked of 'questionable judgment'. The Wanderers rubbed their hands.

Even so, the University almost won. More than once they carried play into the Wanderers' goalmouth, but tried to go through the middle instead of crossing from wide out. Exposed at the back, they let Charles Wollaston run through to score with his left foot 'entirely owing to the absence of the man between the posts' and had to wait a year for revenge (in the quarter-final) on the way to winning the Cup, by which time Kirke Smith, who never got a winner's medal, was making plans to become a vicar (he was ordained in 1875).

Gary Sobers was the greatest all-round cricketer of all time (whisper it within earshot of anything Beefy). A genuinely great batsman (8032 Test runs at 57.78, 26 centuries), dangerous left-arm seamer or spinner (235 wickets) and brilliant close fielder (109 catches), he led the West Indies to three successive series wins by sheer example.

Especially prodigious in England in 1966, he scored 722 runs at 103.14 and took 20 wickets in a 3-1 win. In the second Test, with the West Indies only 11 ahead and five wickets down, he coaxed his cousin David Holford through an unbroken partnership of 274 which saved the match, scoring 163 not out himself. The only time he failed, caught first ball in the last innings of the last Test, England won by an innings. A colossus with bad knees.

So when England went to the Caribbean in 1967–68, more of the same was expected. It didn't happen, partly because the herculean toil had taken its toll, partly because the great player wasn't the greatest tactical captain . . .

Foot in mouth

"Liverpool . . . under their captain Emlyn Jones."
PRINCE MICHAEL OF KENT *(presenting BBC Sports Personality of the Year)*

42

England arrived with a 'new' one of their own, having given the job back to dear old Colin Cowdrey after sacking Brian Close, (who'd won six of his seven Tests as captain) for alleged slow play in a county match. Irony here, because England under Cowdrey now proceeded to occupy the crease and bowl without hurrying, making no obvious attempt to win any of the Tests.

The first three were drawn, England scoring 568 in the first, 449 in the third, hanging on in the second (68-8) after severe crowd trouble. In the fourth, they replied to a total of 526 with 404 of their own, leaving the West Indies not enough time to score a reasonable total then bowl England out.

The thought of a fourth consecutive draw, achieved by the same negative approach as the first three, seems to have been too much for Sobers. It wasn't the way he (or Close . . .) played the game. When the West Indies' second innings reached 92-2, he declared.

It still looks probably the most desperate decision of its kind in Test cricket. He challenged England to score 215 in 3½ hours, which would have been controversial with a full-strength attack but was sheer madness with a line-up whose only strike bowler, Charlie Griffith, was too injured to bowl. Sobers was left with two frontline spinners, his own left-arm medium pace, and two part-

Below: *When Cowdrey's hit on the pads, Sobers (at leg slip) launches an appeal, but too late to save the series* (Popperfoto)

timers. Admittedly one of these, Basil Butcher, had taken 5-34 in the first innings, but that had been a complete one-off and Butcher did nothing in the second.

Even against this job lot, the England captain had to be persuaded to pick up the gauntlet (Ray Illingworth once wrote that Cowdrey could never make up his mind whether to call heads or tails). His senior pros, Edrich, Boycott and Barrington, persuaded him it was too good to miss, England lost only three wickets in winning with three minutes to spare, held on by their fingernails in the last Test, and took the rubber 1-0. Sobers, who never won another series as captain, was the last West Indies skipper to lose one against England (2-0 in 1969).

When the Orange Free State packed down for the last scrum of the match, they were within seconds of becoming the only team to beat the 1974 British Lions: they led 9-7 three minutes into injury time, they had the put-in, and their scrum had been solid throughout.

However, while the Lions were conceding the scrummage by knocking on after a line-out, the Free State lock Stoffel Botha was almost knocked out as he came back in defence. Even before that, his face had looked like a drink-and-drive poster, head bandaged to staunch a cut eye (the Lions used some ugly tactics on that tour). Now, badly concussed, he tried to stand but couldn't, and had to be helped off to allow the scrum to take place.

The Free State needed only to heel the ball from their own put-in then kick to touch to win the game, but their captain Jake Swart tried to do it with only seven men in the scrum, against probably the best set of forwards the Lions had ever sent abroad: the likes of Cotton, McLauchlan, McBride and Mervyn Davies had stampeded through the previous 13 matches.

Swart could have called up an eighth man if he'd stopped to think. For a substitute to be allowed on, Botha had to be examined by a doctor – and no doctor on earth would have pronounced him fit to carry on. Swart didn't call for a doctor – or pull one or two of his backs into the scrum. He simply packed down with the other six forwards close to their own try-line.

Foot in mouth
"Before the game our dressing room was like Dunkirk before they went over the trenches."
JOHN SILLETT

The Lions, with a firmer grasp on things, went for an eight-man shove. They shot the Free State scrummage backwards, Davies gave the ball to Gareth Edwards, who made what ground he could before throwing a pass over his shoulder hoping support was on its way. JJ Williams caught the ball, laid it down over the line, and grinned all over his face as Stoffel Botha put his head in his hands. The Lions won 11-9 and went through the tour unbeaten.

WG Grace on winning the toss: 'Always bat.' Yes, doc, but if the wicket looks ideal for bowling? 'Think about it. Then always bat.'

By 1975 Mike Denness was on probation. After Lillee and Thomson had traumatised the England team he captained in Australia, he was given one last chance, against the same opposition the following summer.

Well, two chances really. The first World Cup, in which England ran Australia close in the semi-final, and the first Test a month later. At Edgbaston he went out for the toss, won it, and lost everything. He asked Ian Chappell to bat.

True, it was an overcast morning, not bad for bowling – but it was surely the decision of a captain who wanted to postpone the inevitable bombardment. In this case, fortune might have favoured the brave: the weather forecast mentioned rain, and Denness took the risk of leaving his batsmen at the mercy of a wet wicket. Sure enough.

Australia made 359 before the skies opened, dismissed England for 101, won by an innings and 85 with a day to spare, took the series by that one Test to nil, and kept the Ashes. Denness didn't play for England again.

In November 1986, having already lost to South Australia, England struggled to draw with a Western Australian XI that bowled them out for 152. The Australian selectors promptly rushed WA's two left-arm seamers, Chris Matthews and the 6ft 8in Bruce Reid, into the Test team.

Four days later on the same ground, despite an attack that had only nine Tests behind it (Geoff Lawson's doubtful stamina kept him out), Allan Border had no hesitation in inviting Mike Gatting to bat, a decision that cost Australia the series.

Matthews, nervous in his first Test, bowled short and wide, Reid took 1-86, England made 456, cruised in by eight wickets, and won the series more easily than 2-1 suggests.

And a versa vice: a captain who batted first when he should have fielded.

In 1946, New Zealand met Australia for the first time, a one-off Test in Wellington on a rain-affected pitch. Walter Hadlee (Richard's father) chose to bat, Australia declared at only 199-8 when their turn came – and won by an innings and 103! New Zealand, all out for 42 and 54, didn't play Australia again till 1973.

Replying to Northamptonshire's first innings total of 294 in 1979, Worcestershire had made 146-6 when Norman Gifford, trying to squeeze a result out of a match ruined by rain, declared the innings closed.

To avoid the follow-on, a county has to finish less than 150 runs behind. Gifford declared 148 behind, hoping to be set a sporting target by Northants' captain Jim Watts. Good thinking, Norman.

However, when an entire day's play has been washed out, the follow-on figure drops to 100. Watts gleefully sent Worcesterhire straight back in. Bad thinking, Norman.

Gifford's batsmen spared his blushes – and almost spoiled a good tale – by holding out for a draw.

In their first match of the 1978 Five Nations championship, Scotland were 12-9 down in injury time at Lansdowne Road when they were awarded a close-range penalty. The simple kick would have guaranteed a draw, but the Scottish captain Doug Morgan decided to go for a winning try by running the ball.

The crowd applauded the attempt, but must have been laughing with relief. Neither side had looked like scoring a try, and Scotland didn't manage one now. Ireland held out to win their only points of the season.

Scotland didn't score any at all. Morgan, retained as captain for the three remaining matches, wasn't capped again after his derring-do rebounded on a team short of confidence and they suffered the first Scottish whitewash for ten years.

With the entire trophy cabinet up for grabs at the end of the 1990 Five Nations series – Calcutta Cup, Championship, Triple Crown, Grand Slam – England were expected not so much to grab as to casually load into the hatchback. While Scotland had been winning by only three points in Ireland and four in Wales, Carling's army had simply looked a class above, scoring 11 tries. Some of the interplay by the backs, who'd scored 9 of them, was as good as anything ever seen in the championship.

At Murrayfield, however, the thoroughbreds ran smack into the Scottish back row, which hovered on the limits of offside throughout the match and harassed everything that moved. Jeremy Guscott's fine try apart, the England backs were never allowed to feature. Still, the forwards were too strong to be held back indefinitely. They applied so much pressure that the Scots were forced to concede penalties inside their own 22, well within range of Simon Hodgkinson's boot.

It had been a trusty piece of footwear all season, kicking 39 points at the end of an economical little leg action. It kicked another three here, but that was too little too late.

Before half-time, Hodgkinson hadn't been allowed to take any of those close-range penalties. It looked from a distance as if the domination of the England tight forwards had gone to the head of the pack leader, the peppery hooker Brian Moore. He, and not Will Carling, seemed to be making the decisions to run the ball instead of letting Hodgkinson go for goal. Even if Carling was more in charge than it looked, those kicks should nevertheless have been taken. Admittedly England were playing into the wind in the first half, but the posts were *so* close . . .

The Scots led 9-4 at the interval, scored an opportunist try soon after it, and held on to take all the glittering prizes 13-7. The following year, England beat them at Twickenham and won the Grand Slam themselves (Hodgkinson kicked a record 63 points), then did it again in 1992 – but for Moore's rush of blood (and Carling's acquiescence), a record three in a row.

OH, REF

and Oh, Ump

The 1877 University Boat Race is down as a dead heat in the record books, but it's not as simple as that. It became the most famous race of all.

Cambridge reached Hammersmith Bridge first, but the bigger Oxford crew soon began to haul them in, making lighter of the choppy conditions. At Chiswick Eyot they were level, at Chiswick church two-thirds of a length ahead. When they had to veer to avoid a barge that had strayed onto the course at near the Mortlake brewery, Cambridge were able to get back to within half a length. At the line, they were close – but definitely not close enough. The Oxford number four, Willie Grenfell, was level with the Cambridge number two, and no-one in either boat was in any doubt: a win for Oxford by perhaps five feet.

There was one small problem. The umpire, Joseph Chitty, couldn't see the finish judge, 'Honest John' Phelps, in the logjam of boats at the end. When he was eventually found, Phelps gave his verdict: a dead heat.

The wonder isn't that he made the wrong decision but that he was able to offer one at all. For a start, he'd never seen a close finish before and didn't know what to look for. More importantly, he'd positioned himself so far away that he could barely see the boats at all. On top of which, his eyesight wasn't what it had been (he was over 70); it was said that he was blind in one eye!

Poor Phelps later became the butt of music hall jokes, which portrayed him as having had a nip too many to keep out the cold, as falling asleep under a bush, as saying 'dead heat to Oxford by five feet'. It wasn't entirely his own fault. No-one had thought to provide a post to help his judgement. One was in place for the following year's race and has been used ever since.

Not surprisingly, Honest John didn't officiate at any more Boat Races. The 1877 edition was the only one to end in a 'dead heat'. Oxford made sure there were no arguments the following year by finishing 10 lengths clear.

The England rugby team regularly reaped the benefit of dubious decisions before the turn of the century, most glaringly against the touring New Zealand Native XV, the so-called Maoris, at Blackheath in 1889.

When the NZ full-back William Warbrick started to run the ball from behind his own line, he saw he was under challenge from Harry Bedford, and touched down to concede a five-yard scrum – only for the English referee GR Hill to award a try to England

Foot in mouth
"Oxford is in front. No, Cambridge. No, Oxford. I don't know who's in front: either Oxford or Cambridge."
JOHN SNAGGE
(1952 Boat Race)

47

when Bedford fell on the ball! Later in the first half, Bedford scored another try, again after one of the New Zealanders, HH Lee, had touched down first. In the second half, Drewy Stoddart, the famous centre who also captained England at cricket, scored a try – then lost his shorts when tackled by TR Ellison.

While the players formed a circle round Stoddart as he adjusted his clothing, Frank Evershed picked the ball up and claimed a try in the corner. When the New Zealanders remonstrated with the referee, Evershed took the ball round to the posts, where Hill awarded the try! John Willie Sutcliffe, who also kept goal for England, kicked the only conversion of the match while three of the Natives walked off the field.

England were awarded five tries and won 7-0 (worth 27-0 now).

At Lansdowne Road in 1882, after England had beaten Ireland in the first seven rugby internationals between the two, an evenly contested match ended in uproar. After tries by WN (Wilfrid Nash) Bolton and Robert Hunt had given England the lead, Ireland equalised when Johnston crossed the line in the last few minutes.

The conversion was entrusted to RE (Robert Edward) McLean, who clipped it home – only to have it disallowed by the umpire, a physician called Nugent. Everyone else at the ground had seen the ball go over the bar and between the posts, but the doctor had ordered and that was that. It was the first time Ireland had avoided defeat against England, but they had to wait another five years to beat them for the first time.

In 1903, Reggie and Laurie Doherty beat another pair of brothers, Bob and George Wrenn, to send Britain into the last day of the Davis Cup challenge round 2-1 ahead. The Americans would have to win both singles on the last day to keep the trophy.

The matches were played simultaneously, on adjoining courts so that the players on one could hear the scores from the other. At one stage, both matches were level in the fifth set: Laurie 4-4 with Bill Larned, Reggie 3-3 with Bob Wrenn – whereupon Laurie, 15-40 down, served and went to the net, where Larned passed him to win the game.

Then, as Larned changed ends to get ready to serve for the match (and put intolerable pressure on the fragile Reggie next door), Laurie politely asked the umpire if his last service had been in (no question of Little Do trying anything on: he was the most gentlemanly of gentlemen). The umpire turned to the linesman – who wasn't there.

The story goes that he'd gone off to catch a boat, and in the excitement no-one had noticed him. No-one noticed?! Didn't he have a tongue in his head? An arm to raise? *Please sir, may I be excused?* Penny for your thoughts, Mr Larned.

The referee, James Dwight, ordered the point to be replayed, Laurie won it, and the set 7-5. Soon afterwards, despite an injured shoulder, Reggie beat Wrenn 6-4. Britain won the cup for the first time, the USA didn't regain it till ten years later.

In 1927, Big Bill Tilden was having his usual troubles with the French, including that incredible Wimbledon semi-final against Henri Cochet (see STRIKING IT POOR). Before that, he took on the Musketeers in their own backyard, beating Cochet in straight sets in the semi-final of the French championships, giving René Lacoste (11 years his junior) a run for it in the final.

On a fiercely hot day, he could have claimed the match when the frail Lacoste was hit by cramp in the fourth set. Instead (those were the days) he gave him time to recover, lost the set, but recovered well enough to serve for the match at 9-8 in the fifth.

At match point, he fired one of his patented cannonball serves, which Lacoste could only acknowledge with a nod of the head. Both knew the serve had been good, as did the crowd. The applause for Big Bill, always a favourite in Europe, was unreserved.

Then, as the two moved in to shake hands at the net, they heard the serve called out. Tilden turned imperiously to upbraid the linesman – who was Henri Cochet! He'd replaced a regular official who'd been hit by sunstroke. Tilden always found Cochet difficult as a player. As an official, he was unbeatable. Big Bill, who had two match points in all, lost the last three games and never won the French title.

Foot in mouth
"And Dickie Bird standing there with his neck between his shoulders."
BRIAN JOHNSTON

Even without their injured playmaker, the great Alec James, Arsenal were expected to beat Newcastle in the 1932 FA Cup final. No James, but still Jack and John: David Jack the lean skilful England centre-forward led the line expertly in the final, Bob John the Welsh international half-back headed Arsenal into an early lead. With only a few minutes to go to half-time, Arsenal were in comfortable control.

Then the Newcastle centre-half Dave Davidson hit a speculative long pass out to the right wing. Jimmy Richardson gave chase but the ball was going too fast. As it went out of play over the goal line, the Arsenal defenders relaxed and began to turn away for the goal kick. Richardson got a late foot in, hooked it across, and watched his centre-forward Jack Allen, unsurprisingly unmarked, head it in at the near post.

It wasn't a goal. Couldn't have been. The ball had gone briefly but clearly over the line. Arsenal turned to the referee, Percy Harper, only to see him moving back to the middle.

A contested equaliser, awarded so close to half-time, would set any team back. It was certainly the beginning of the end for Arsenal. In the second half, they switched Cliff Bastin to the right and Jack to centre-forward – but the latter missed a sitter and Allen scored his second goal, the winner.

Instead of admitting the decisive mistake, Harper stood his ground: 'As God is my judge, the man was in play.' True, but photographs and film prove that the ball wasn't. 'I was eight yards away.' Not so. He can be seen quite clearly, standing several yards outside the penalty area. 'I do not mind what other people say.' Just as well.

Arsenal won the Cup four years later.

Above: *How's that for a let-off? The Don cashes in on his luck in 1946–47* (Popperfoto)

When the Ashes rivalry resumed after the last war, there was some suspicion that the great Bradman was past his best. Certainly he looked completely out of form in his first innings of the first Test, at Brisbane in 1946.

When Arthur Morris was dismissed for only 2 in his first Test innings, Bradman came in with the score at 9-1 and played so badly that Sid Barnes had to protect him from Alec Bedser, whom the Don had never faced before. Soon after Barnes had been caught by Bedser to leave Australia 46-2, Bradman attacked a wide delivery from Bill Voce, the left-armer who'd partnered Larwood in the 1932–33 Bodyline series but was now 37. Aiming to cut the ball square on the offside, Bradman edged it at chest height straight to second slip, where Jack Ikin never looked like dropping it.

It was such an obvious catch that at first the England fielders didn't bother to appeal. Norman Yardley, in the gully, remembered watching the ball off the pitch, onto the bat, and into Ikin's hands. No question of a bump ball. Ikin waited for Bradman to start off towards the pavilion. When he didn't move, England appealed. Australian umpire George Borwick gave the Australian captain not out.

A staggering, demoralising decision. It seemed impossible for a bump ball to have gone shoulder-high at such a pace as to turn Ikin round when he caught it. It *had* to have touched the bat last.

Off the field, Bill O'Reilly (Bradman's great leg-spinner from the Thirties) and Sydney broadcaster Clif Cary were just two of many who had no doubts ('It was a legitimate catch absolutely'). On it, the England captain Wally Hammond, a magnificent batsman who'd been under the Don's shadow throughout the

Thirties, passed Bradman at the end of the over and mentioned something to the effect that this was 'a fine XXXX way to start a series.'

It certainly was for Bradman. On 28 when he was caught by Ikin, he went on to top-score with 187 and share a record third-wicket partnership of 276 with Lindsay Hassett, then make 234 in the next Test. Australia won the series 3-0 and retained the Ashes.

Although Real Madrid were waiting for the winners, the 1962 European Cup semi between Benfica and Tottenham looked very much the 'real' final. The holders against the winners of the Double in England, both reinforced by brilliant strikers: Eusebio da Silva Ferreira and James Peter Greaves. Neither scored in the semi-final – but Greavsie, by rights, should have been the matchwinner.

In the first leg, in Lisbon, Tottenham were caught in the blast of a typical Benfica 'storm', Aguas and José Augusto scoring within the first 20 minutes. Bobby Smith pulled one back, but José Augusto headed his second: 3-1, enough to see them through the second leg.

It shouldn't have been. Tottenham had two goals wrongly disallowed by the Swiss referee Daniel Mellet. First, Greaves was given offside despite beating the full-back, then with nine minutes left he crossed for Smith to score his second. Mellet gave the goal, then disallowed it even though Greaves had pulled the ball back: it *couldn't* have been offside.

In the return, Aguas scored after 15 minutes and Tottenham, foundering on the rocks of Germano and Costa Pereira, won only 2-1 (Greaves had another goal disallowed). They would probably have beaten an ageing Real in the final. Benfica did it instead, 5-3 after being 3-2 down at half-time.

The following year, while Benfica were reaching the European Cup final for the third consecutive year, losing unluckily and controversially to Milan, Tottenham found their level by taking the Cup-Winners' Cup, the first British club to collect a European trophy.

The 1974 British Lions went into the fourth Test, the last match of their South African tour, having won all their previous 21. This time, missing Gordon Brown in the second row, they struggled to establish any real authority and were being held 13-13 (Piet Cronje had scored South Africa's only try of the series) when John Williams set off on one of his typical surges through the middle.

This was the high point of JPR's international career. Far and away the best full-back in the world, perhaps of all time, he hadn't missed a tackle all tour (he dropped a high ball, just one, and worried about it for days afterwards) and his running from the back had brought him three tries. Now he came inside Chris Pope, past Jackie Snyman, took Jan Schlebusch's tackle, and passed to Fergus Slattery, who drove through Cronje's tackle and over the line.

Cronje fell on his back in an attempt to stop Slattery grounding the ball, and succeeded – but for only for a second at most. Then the flanker forced it between Cronje's legs and touched down. The winning try.

Except that referee Max Baise gave a five yard scrum, from which JJ Williams was held just short. South Africa escaped with the draw and treated the 3-0 series defeat as a national holiday.

Why did Baise blow so quickly? To prevent a maul forming, he said. They 'can be dangerous, and I don't like to let them develop'. But there was precious little chance of that with only Hannes Marais anywhere near. 'Other players were arriving quickly,' claimed Baise – but not that quickly, not so that he had to blow after just two seconds. The decision cost the Lions the first clean sweep in a series against South Africa since 1891.

Keith Butcher once awarded Everton a penalty when the free kick should have gone to West Brom. Before another match, he didn't realise both teams were wearing the same colour until a linesman broke the news. He later admitted he'd been unable to tell the difference between red and yellow cards. A fully qualified League referee, he was colour blind.

Although England's defence of the Five Nations championship, won by the 1980 Grand Slam team, foundered in the very first match, lost 21-19 in Cardiff, they went into the last with a chance of sharing the title.

France had won all three so far, but England, playing at Twickenham and probably the better side, had reasons for optimism. In the first half, facing a gale, they were only 3-0 down and holding out well when France won a lineout on the left.

As soon as the ball went out of play, scrum-half Pierre Berbizier snatched another from a ball boy and threw it in to his captain Jean-Pierre Rives before a lineout could be formed. Rives gave the ball to the other flanker Pierre Lacans, who touched down.

Now, the rules are very clear about it. A quick throw-in can only be taken with the same ball that went out of play. The England captain Bill Beaumont mentioned this to the referee, Alan Hosie of Scotland, who ignored it and awarded the try that put France 9-0 ahead. The decision cost England a share of the title and presented France with the Grand Slam: they used the wind to lead 16-0 at half-time and held on to win by 4 points.

In their last match of the 1989 international championship, England led 9-6 at half-time: two penalties and a drop goal by Rob Andrew to two penalties by Paul Thorburn, the Welsh captain, who kicked off to the open side to start the second half and had his reward when Rory Underwood knocked on.

From the scrum, fly-half Paul Turner banged in another high kick, and Underwood made another mistake, thinking of passing to Jonathan Webb instead of kicking to touch. The ball went loose, winger Arthur Emyr kicked on, Mike Hall gave chase and fell on the ball over the England line. The referee gave the try.

At the time, it didn't look certain that Hall had put any downward pressure on the ball, an impression confirmed by television replays. The try-that-wasn't saved Wales from a white-wash and cost England the title as well as a first win in Cardiff since 1963.

In the same year, at the beginning of the following season, another refereeing error did Underwood no favours. Against Fiji at Twickenham, he scored two tries in the first seven minutes, three before half-time, five in all: a share in the world record for the most scored by a single player in an international match.

Not bad, deserved better. When he dived in yet again at the corner, he put the ball down over the line just before being bundled into touch. The linesman and Irish referee Brian Stirling gave a line-out. Again, TV confirmed that Underwood had scored before going over the sideline. He would have been – is – the only player to score six tries in an international.

The first Test against the 1993 All Blacks was only two minutes old when the Lions aged considerably. Ieuan Evans went up for a high ball deep in his right-hand corner and was driven back over the line by Frank Bunce. Australian referee Brian Kinsey awarded a try.

Now, although Bunce had got his hands to the ball, Evans' didn't seem too far away (he later claimed he didn't let go throughout). The referee, faced with a tangle of bodies going at high speed, must surely have had his doubts, and should therefore have given the defending side the benefit of them. It was the only try of the match.

Above: *Dewi Morris can't believe it as another Kinsey decision brings British rugby to its knees* (Colorsport)

Putting the disappointment behind them, the Lions took control of the game, especially in the loose, where Ben Clarke (a makeshift flanker), Peter Winterbottom and Dean Richards outplayed Jamie Joseph, Zinzan Brooke and the messianic Michael Jones. Full-back and captain Gavin Hastings kicked six penalty goals from eight attempts to put the Lions ahead 18-17.

But Kinsey hadn't finished with them yet. Two minutes from time, Richards tackled Bunce in midfield, a ruck formed above them, and Richards was penalised for not allowing release of the ball. From 42 yards, under great pressure, Grant Fox kicked his fifth penalty goal to win the match 20-18.

How Richards was supposed to have rolled away from the ball with both sets of forwards pinning him down was never satisfactorily explained, certainly not to Lions manager Geoff Cooke who thought 'The tackled-ball situation is being refereed very badly over here.' Those refereeing decisions cost the Lions the series: they won the second Test 20-7 before losing the decider.

HANDS OF GOD

In the 1930s, Silvio Piola was the best centre-forward in the world. Tall, aggressive, linchpin of Italy's attack in the 1938 World Cup (five goals, including two in the final), he looked – and knew he was – every inch a star.

Twinkled against England, too. Or at least the glare dazzled the referee. At the San Siro in 1939, Italy equalised five minutes into the second half, then Miguel Andreolo put in a high ball which right-back George Male seemed to have covered.

Up went Piola, not with the brylcreemed head but the velvet fist. The ball went past Vic Woodley, the follow-through gave Male a black eye, German referee Peco Bauwens awarded the goal.

Justice was done when Stanley Matthews crossed, Len Goulden's shot was blocked, Willie Hall knocked it in. It was the world champions' 26th game without defeat, and the dodgiest of Piola's 30 goals in 34 internationals.

In 1952, he was recalled after an absence of more than five years as captain in the 1-1 draw with England. It was his last cap, he was 38, and didn't have a hand in Italy's goal.

After losing their opening match in the 1978 World Cup qualifiers (2-0 in Prague, Andy Gray sent off), Scotland needed a little luck, got it when Ian Evans' own goal gave them a 1-0 win over Wales at Hampden, then beat Czechoslovakia in the return, and went into the last match, against Wales, needing only a draw to qualify.

Moving the game to Anfield turned a home match for Wales into a Scottish singalong. Already without Leighton James, the Welsh were forced back from the start, Dai Davies making a fine save from Dalglish. Somehow they held on, had a chance to go ahead through Peter Sayer, and looked the better side up to half-time and beyond, forcing Allan Rough to a fingertip save on the hour.

Soon afterwards, Willie Johnston put a long throw-in into the area, a group of players went up for it, one of them used a hand, French referee Robert Wurtz gave a penalty against David Jones. Television replays fingered Joe Jordan.

Don Masson sent Davies the wrong way from the spot, Dalglish headed a second, Scotland went to the finals, Wales haven't reached them since 1958. In 1982 Jordan became the only British player to score in the final stages of three World Cups. In 1981, a few years too late, he was sent off against Wales.

The goal that sent Scotland to the 1986 finals, again at Wales' expense, was scored from the penalty spot.

After stumbling about in the first two matches of the 1986 tournament (losing 1-0 to Portugal, drawing 0-0 with Morocco, having Ray Wilkins sent off), England came alive with two 3-0 wins (and five Lineker goals) to reach the quarter-finals.

Against Argentina, a one-man band with several good second fiddles, they played out a tense, undistinguished first half and were still holding their own when Steve Hodge sliced an attempted clearance back towards his own goal.

The two captains went up for it, Shilton slightly too slowly but Maradona still unlikely to get there first. At the last second, using his head, he put his hand up, the ball bounced in, and the Tunisian referee Ali Ben Nasser gave the goal. Photographs show Maradona palming the loose change, with Shilts' fist inches away from where fair-minded individuals would like to see it.

Four minutes later, Maradona scored a brilliant second, two more in the semi-final, and put Jorge Burruchaga through for the winning goal in the final. No World Cup has ever been so completely dominated by one player.

Four years later, the little tear jerk was at it

Above: The Hand of the Baskervilles (Allsport)

again. First in an Italian league match, then against the USSR in the World Cup finals.

Both teams had lost their opening match, the Soviets 2-0, Argentina shockingly to Cameroon. Now, after only 12 minutes, Igor Dobrovolsky took a corner on the left, Oleg Kuznetsov flicked it on, and Maradona (playing on his home club ground) handled to stop the ball going in. Swedish referee Erik Fredriksson didn't see it.

Argentina won 2-0, sneaked their way through the quarters and semis on penalties, and came within five minutes of taking West Germany to extra-time in the final, after which poor little Diego couldn't keep back the tears. Fit to break your heart. Dear me, yes.

From 1956 to 1981, England's record against Brazil read P12 W1 D4 L7. Since then, surprisingly: P5 W2 D3 L0. Mind you, it's always been pretty close.

Never more so than at Wembley in 1990. After 36 minutes, England went ahead through a strange little header by Lineker from the first corner of the match. In the second half, Luiz Antonio Correa da Costa lived up to his nickname (Muller) by going past Shilton and shooting into the empty net.

'Into' was the operative word. The ball clearly crossed the line before Stuart Pearce clearly handled it. Surrounded by furious Brazilians, the East German referee Klaus Peschel took out the yellow card, didn't use it, consulted a linesman, and gave a throw-in! England beat Brazil at home for the first time since 1956.

OFFICIALS WHO DIDN'T MEASURE UP

Organisation at the 1900 Olympics was haphazard to say the least. The athletics events, for instance, were held in the middle of the Bois de Boulogne, and discus throwers had to go for accuracy as well as distance: a large tree grew in the middle of what passed for an arena.

The pole vault was a glaring example. When three of the leading Americans objected to competing on a Sunday, officials agreed to change the day. Two of the vaulters, Bascom Johnson and Charlie Dvorak, turned up anyway (their lack of faith in the organisers turned out to be well founded) but were sent back with assurances.

Predictably, the officials simply changed their minds. The event *was* held on the Sunday, without Johnson, Dvorak, and the other objector Dan Horton. Irving Baxter, still on the field after winning the high jump, won this too, the only athlete ever to achieve this double in the Olympics – but at the mediocre height of 3.30m (10ft 10in).

Later, as a small sop to the three absentees, another pole vault competition was held. Horton (3.45) won from Dvorak (3.40), both clearing heights well in excess of Baxter's effort – but neither's listed as an official Olympic medallist for 1900. Dvorak took the gold four years later, but Horton never won an Olympic medal.

In 1903, 5-1 joint favourites Renzo and Set Fair fought out a close finish to the 6-furlong Peel Handicap, but Renzo was the clear winner, albeit by only a head. The spectators saw it, the jockeys saw it, even Set Fair's trainer had no doubts. Only one person missed it. The chief judge, who was standing at the wrong finishing post.

The stewards fined him £20 and re-ran the race at the end of the day. In an unfair ending, Set Fair beat Renzo – by a head.

The French athletics team who arrived in Los Angeles for the 1932 Olympics found themselves among barbarians. Horror of horrors, a land in the grip of Prohibition. Defiantly they argued that although alcohol was illegal in the USA it formed a vital part of the French sportsman's diet – and won their case.

Several cases actually, if the conduct of their discus throwers was anything to go by. In between throws, Jules Noël and Paul

In the final of the 1904 Olympic 400 metres hurdles, Harry Hillman held off Frank Waller by 0.2 seconds to win the second of his three gold medals. At first, it looked as if his time of 53.0 had shattered Godfrey Shaw's world record of 57.2. Then it was realised that he'd knocked over one of the hurdles, which invalidated records at the time. Then, more pertinently, it was pointed out that he'd beaten Shaw's time by such a margin because officials had laid out the wrong hurdles: they were six inches too low.

Winter were seen making trips to the stadium tunnel, where they quaffed champagne with other team members.

Thus fortified, they challenged strongly for the medals. In fact, Noël's fourth throw landed beyond the leading marker of American John Anderson, far enough for the gold medal.

Far enough, that is, if the discus officials had kept even half an eye on what they were supposed to be doing. Instead, they were looking the other way, engrossed in the pole vault, where Bill Miller was holding off the Japanese challenge by a single centimetre.

Amid great embarrassment, Noël was awarded an extra throw, but the champagne was either beginning to work or had already done its best, and he finished only fourth, behind the bronze medallist Winter and two Americans, including one with a French name. All sorrows were presumably drowned.

American sprinter Ralph Metcalfe had a slow, lumbering start and was never properly coached in his life (compare film of his style with that of the immaculately tutored Jesse Owens). Nevertheless, for a number of years he was probably the fastest runner in the world, winner of the Olympic silver medal in the 100 metres of 1932 (by very few inches) and 1936 (behind Owens).

In the 1932 200, his fast finish gave him every chance of turning the tables – but he was too far behind coming into the straight and finished third behind Eddie Tolan, who did the double, and George Simpson. After the race, it was discovered that officials had made Metcalfe dig his starting holes more than a yard further back than he should have, enough to cost him the silver and quite possibly the gold.

He refused all offers of a re-run and was probably rewarded in heaven (as well as the 1936 sprint relay).

Foot in mouth
"Well, there it is: the judges have given a draw, but we'll be back in a couple of minutes to talk to the loser."
REG GUTTERIDGE

At the end of the 1932 steeplechase (it was a vintage year for Olympic errors) Volmari Iso-Hollo of Finland finished 40 yards clear of the field, only to find the judge responsible for counting the laps (who was deputising for the usual official) telling him there was another one to go.

Iso-Hollo, the favourite, later the world record holder, knew this was wrong but ran the extra lap anyway – and won by more than 70 yards.

But the error affected the minor placings. Joe McCluskey of the USA had sprinted in to finish second, and was too tired to hold off Britain's Tom Evenson on the appendix lap. A re-run was offered, but McCluskey declined and settled for the bronze. It was the only 3460 metre steeplechase ever run in a major championship.

A similar mistake affected the placings in the men's 10 000 metres at the 1987 world championships. With two laps still to go, the lap counter showed only one. This made no difference to the winner (Paul Kipkoech, 10 seconds clear in a championship record that still stands) or the runner-up (local hero Francesco Panetta, who later won the steeplechase), but certainly confused the fight for third place. The likes of Martti Vainio and Arturo Barrios virtually stopped running (Vainio didn't finish the race), allowing the well-known fast finisher Hansjörg Kunze to sprint home for the bronze.

At the finish of the 1938 Natal Marathon, Johannes Coleman arrived at the Alexander Park stadium in Pietermaritzburg with a big lead – not surprisingly, given that he was then probably the best Marathon runner in the world, sixth in the 1936 Olympics, fourth in 1948, Commonwealth champion (by nearly seven minutes) in 1938.

As he entered the stadium, his own watch showed that he'd been running only 2 hours 23 minutes. Even a very slow finish would leave him well inside Olympic champion Sohn Kee Chung's world record of 2 hrs 26 mins 42 secs. Coleman padded round the track – and found that he'd arrived earlier than the chief timekeeper had anticipated: the worthy gent was still in the tea room. Coleman never did set an official world record.

When Donald McNab Robertson and Squire Yarrow entered the White City stadium at the end of the 1946 AAA Marathon, they found the place cluttered with officials, runners, and heavy barriers: the steeplechase final was still going on.

McNab Robertson, a famous finisher at the end of long-distance races, was slowed down so much by all the confusion that he lost to Yarrow by 0.2 seconds, easily the narrowest margin in any AAA Marathon.

A photo-finish picture taken after the 1948 Olympic women's 200m shows that the original judges were wrong to award the bronze medal to Audrey Patterson of the USA; she finished fourth behind

In the 1936 Olympic boxing, South African lightweight Tom Hamilton-Brown lost a split decision to Carlos Lillo of Chile. Or so it was first announced. Then it transpired that one of the judges had put his marks for Hamilton-Brown in Lillo's column and vice versa!

Someone found the South African and told him he'd won the fight after all. Too late. HB had suffocated his sorrows under a mountain of food and was now five pounds over the limit. Next day, still overweight, he had to be disqualified. Lillo went through in his place and reached the quarter-finals.

Foot in mouth

"Mansell, Senna, Prost. Put them in any order and you end up with the same three drivers."
DEREK WARWICK

the famous Australian sprinter-hurdler Shirley Strickland. Despite the evidence, the records have never been changed and Strickland's still credited with a total of seven medals (an all-time record she shares with Irina Szewinska) instead of her rightful eight.

The greatest of all Olympic swimming controversies came out of the men's 100 metres freestyle final of 1960. John Devitt of Australia, silver medallist from the previous Games, finished second again, this time to Lance Larson of the USA. The paper tapes at the end of the pool, the photo-finish cameras, and above all the electronic timers (Larson 55.1, Devitt 55.2) all proved it.

Astonishingly, despite all this evidence and the fact that two of the officials who were appointed to decide second place placed Devitt behind Larson, two of the first-place judges voted for Devitt as the winner.

Worse still, for some reason still not satisfactorily explained, the chief judge (who, according to the rules, had no say in the matter) awarded the gold medal to Devitt – after changing Larson's time to 55.2! Years of protest made no difference to the 'result'.

Right: *For me, it was all about bronze. While Larson and Devitt can't believe their luck, Manuel dos Santos looks happy with third place*
(Popperfoto)

At match point in the first round at Wimbledon in 1964, Clark Graebner hit the ball out and went to the net to congratulate Abe Segal. His shot had been almost two feet out, which was just as well because there was no call: the line judge was asleep!

Afterwards, Dorothy Cavis Brown claimed she'd had only a single gin at lunchtime, plus a little olive oil to line the stomach. It's just that she'd been feeling tired for several days now (watching Segal play probably didn't help).

The photograph of Cavis Brown, arms folded, legs crossed, head on one side, became one of the most famous Wimbledon visuals. She didn't officiate there again.

The best runners were all packed into the second heat of the 5000m at the 1978 Commonwealth Games: Henry Rono, Brendan Foster, Rod Dixon, Mike McLeod. As they reached the start of the last lap, one of the officials dropped a clanger. The clanger. As the runners approached, he rang the bell – and it fell off.

Before the 1988 Olympics, someone had the brainwave of using two boxing rings in the hall at the same time. It didn't seem to have occurred to anyone that the bell ending a round in one ring could be heard in the other.

Near the end of the first round of a light-welterweight fight between Todd Foster of the USA and Chun Jin Chul of South Korea, the bell sounded in the other ring while there were still 17 seconds left in this one. The referee seemed about to end the round, and Chun started to go back to his corner, whereupon Foster, quite within his rights, hit him with a big left hook.

The referee began counting over Chun (who seemed to be pretending to be knocked out in an attempt to have Foster disqualified), then changed his mind and went over to the judges, who subsequently ordered a rematch, which Foster won the following day.

Although there seems to be no truth in the rumour that a horse called Hoof Hearted was allowed to race, Weatherbys have let a few iffy monikers slip through the net.

Snurge, for example, the 1990 St Leger winner, would never have been so called if officials had had access to the Dictionary of Slang and Unconventional English.

The classy hurdler Kybo was in fact KYBO: Keep Your Bowels Open (the advice given to the owner, Isidore Kerman, by his mother).

Biganard ran in novice races in 1991. Who Gives A Donald (1989) had his roots in rhyming slang (Donald = Donald Duck =), and Foxtrot Oscar came from the police radio code (FO = F Off).

IT'S OFF!

Grand National 1993

The 150th Grand National, the 1993 edition of the contentious event, was due to start at 3.50pm. Just under 25 minutes earlier, after Red Rum had been paraded yet again, the 39 runners and riders were led out for the start, which was delayed while police cleared the course of animal rights campaigners and their Stop the Slaughter banner.

At 3.58, chief starter Keith Brown pulled the lever that should have hoisted the starting tape over the horses' heads. But it was a windy day, and at the tail end of the twentieth century the Jockey Club was still starting the most famous steeplechase in the world with 80 yards of tape, which couldn't cope with such an unexpected British phenomenon as the wind.

It blew some of those yards round horses' torsoes and jockeys' necks, and Brown had to wave his red flag (another miracle of the computerised age) to stop the race, but not

Below: The escape goat. Keith Brown leaves Aintree to its own devices (Bob Thomas Sports Photography)

before six horses had reached the first fence.

Mild embarrassment – but there was always a second chance, chaps. At 4.03, Brown tried again. Again the wind flung the tape backwards, this time nearly throttling Judy Davies' horse Formula One and wrapping itself round leading jockey Richard Dunwoody, whose mount was the most aptly named in the race: Won't Be Gone Long.

Again Brown raised his red flag. This time it didn't unfurl and only nine riders held their horses back. As eleven of them charged round the second circuit, the Jockey Club brought all its hi-tec gadgetry to bear: Rodger Farrant and recall judge Ken Evans waved their flags for all they were worth (offers on a postcard), other officials put a cone down in front of the Chair fence!

Wonder of wonders, even this didn't stop all the horses from finishing. John White on Jenny Pitman's Esha Ness crossed the line first before the whole sorry affair was declared null and void and not rerun that year.

While the hapless Brown was being given a police escort through the gauntlet of irate racegoers ('I'll see you in court' said trainer John Upson), the Jockey Club was already looking for scapegoats, finally finding one in Ken Evans, who was paid £28 a day (typical of the industry) for performing one of the most responsible duties in a race worth many millions.

Evans, said the august body, hadn't waved his recall flag. Why, even the jockeys said they hadn't seen it. Evans protested that he'd been flapping away right from the start. Whichever, it was clear that the Jockey Club's employment of retired military personnel had to be looked into (they apparently make up 'the vast majority' of officials on Britain's 59 racecourses; Keith Brown was a captain), as did the use of outdated technology, for want of another word: a long bit of string in place of the starting stalls urged by William Hill and used in national hunt racing in Australia and the USA.

Senior steward Lord Hartington wore even more of a hangdog expression than normal, though most punters thought hanging the dog would be too good for him. The Jokey club they called it.

It was a national scandal (a leader in The Times, no less) and a great day's sport. Leading jockey Peter Scudamore, the top cat riding Captain Dibble, trying to win the race for the first time at the 13th attempt, thought it likely that 'we'll be the laughing stock of the world'. With 300 million watching, you betcha bottom dollar; in this case, £75 million worth of bottom dollars in bets. The country lost £6 million in taxes, the whole crazy industry itself £1 million. Time for someone to clean out its Augean stables.

Don't hold your breath. In August, a working party chaired by Andrew Parker Bowles (a brigadier) produced a 34-page document that recommended drastic all-encompassing action: the use of two flag men! No change, in other words. No need, said the brigadier: 'It won't happen again.'

Still, there was a bright side. This time the North West Animal Rights Coalition could go home satisfied with that notable phenomenon: no dead horses after the people's race.

Above: Dunjumpin. Richard sits it out like everyone else (Bob Thomas Sports Photography)

VERY LITTLE GREY CELLS

competitors who didn't keep their wits about them

George Bentinck was one of the country's most prominent racehorse owners in the middle of the last century, a time of rampant skulduggery in betting circles, which cost him dear in the 1844 Derby when the colt he'd backed, Ratan, was held back by its jockey, the notorious Sam Rogers.

Bentinck doesn't seem to have had much luck with stable staff either. The story goes that, just before one of his horses was due to run, its trainer wrote two notes:

To Bentinck himself: *My lord, the colt is quite fit and has done a rattling gallop. I fancy he is bound to win. Pray back him for all you can on Monday next if only you can get a fair price.*

To a bookmaker: *Joe, the long-legged lord will be at Tattersalls on Monday. Lay him all you can. The horse is a dead one.*

Unfortunately for the trainer, he put the letters in the wrong envelopes.

Sometimes blue blood comes from a very small genetic pool. Count John de Bendern, formerly John de Forest, British Amateur champion in 1932, once hit a shot onto the sloping bank of the brook on the 13th hole at Augusta during the US Masters.

Peculiar problems require radical solutions. Count John took off his right shoe. Then his right sock. Then rolled up his trouser leg to just above the knee. He stood over the ball and practised his swing, looked ahead, looked down, and took up his stance over the ball. Then Count John, a complete aristocrat, put his bare right foot on the bank and his left foot (still in its shoe) in the water.

When golfer Jock Hutchison won the 1921 British Open, it was the first time the claret jug was taken to the USA. Mind you, he'd won it on his home patch: based in America, he was a native of St Andrews. In the first round, he shot a hole-in-one at the eighth and missed another by inches at the next hole.

He won the event courtesy of Roger Wethered, whom he beat by 9 strokes in a play-off. As well as bogeying the last hole on the last round, Wethered had incurred a penalty stroke during the third – by treading on his own ball.

Jacqueline Pung finished a stroke clear of the field at the 1957 women's US Open but didn't win the title. At the 4th hole, she took a 6 but accidentally signed for a 5 and was disqualified. A whip-round by Winged Foot club members raised more than $3000 (almost double the first prize) but it didn't compensate Pung for a title she never won. Betsy Rawls, who finished behind her, was awarded the third of her record four US Opens.

In 1968, a similar oversight decided one of the Majors. A year after winning one at last (the British Open), the popular Argentinian Roberto de Vicenzo holed his putt for a birdie 3 at the 71st hole of the Masters at Augusta.

Then, even more bizarrely than Pung, he signed for the wrong score: a 4 not a 3. The mistake wasn't noticed till after the card had been entered, by which time there was no going back: the phantom extra stroke counted, De Vicenzo lost the Masters to Bob Goalby by that one shot, and never won a second Major.

If there was any doubt in the referee's mind as to which fighter had won the British and Commonwealth heavyweight title bout at Earl's Court in January 1959, one of them removed it for him.

Brian London held up Henry Cooper's hand to acknowledge him as the new champion – only to be informed by referee Ike Powell that there was another round to go. London lost on points and never got the title back.

While Arnold Palmer was making one of his famous charges through the last round of the 1960 US Open, a podgy crewcut 20-year-old was showing the first signs of a heavyweight talent, leading by a stroke with six holes to play.

At the 13th, young Jack Nicklaus maintained his form with two excellent shots, a 3 wood and a delicate 9 iron, to leave him with an uphill putt of 12 feet for the birdie. When he missed it, he left himself an awkward, downhill, but very short putt for his par.

As he settled over it, he saw a dip in his path, a faint depression made by another ball. Not much of an obstacle, but enough to make Jack wonder. Was he allowed to repair the hollow? Would it make much difference if he didn't?

His playing partner was the legendary Ben Hogan, polite enough but reputedly sharp with his replies to daft questions. Nicklaus, unsure if his question were daft or not, couldn't pluck up the nerve to ask it, of Hogan or an official.

If he had, he'd have been told that he had every right to carry out the repair. Instead, he went through with the putt, the ball inevitably touched the cavity, veered, caught the lip of the cup, and stayed out. The dropped stroke cost him the lead, he dropped another at the next, and lost to Palmer's headlong 65. Nicklaus won the event for the first time two years later.

In the third round of the 1960 Olympic final, British record holder Sue Platt fired the javelin out to beyond the 54 metre mark, leaped with joy – and came down to earth beyond the foul line. The

When the world professional snooker championship was revived after seven years, John Pulman's first challenge came from 50-year-old Fred Davis, from whom he'd taken the title in 1957.

The turning point came when Davis, leading 13-11, forgot to nominate a free ball, even though there was no doubt at all as to which one he was going for. It was an unnecessarily harsh rule (the wording was changed in 1976) but Fred knew it, simply forgot it, lost the match 19-16, another against Pulman in 1965 (by only 37-36) and never did win the title back.

throw, which would have won her the silver medal, was given the red flag and she finished 7th. The Commonwealth title two years later was small consolation.

In the quarter-final of the 1980 World Matchplay championship, Nick Faldo led Greg Norman by 6 shots after 25 holes but by only one coming to the 36th and last. The match was played in steady rain, which made all the difference to the final outcome.

The last hole was a long dog-leg, and Norman believed his only chance of squaring the match was to attack for a birdie 4. When he put his second shot in a bunker, then missed his birdie putt from 15 feet, it looked all over. Faldo needed only to get down in two from 8 feet.

Throughout most of the day, both players had been using squeegee boards to push water off the soaking greens. Now Faldo used one on the grass between his ball and the hole, then (the mistake) several feet past.

The squeegee flattened the grass in the direction of the hole, which meant that if Faldo ran his ball past the hole, he'd have to putt back against the grain.

Needless to say, the slick surface took the ball about five feet past, then stopped it short on the way back. He took a 6 and was forced into a sudden-death play-off which he lost at the second extra hole.

Norman went on to beat Sandy Lyle at the very last hole of the final and won the title again in 1983 (beating Faldo in the final) and 1986. Faldo had to wait till 1989 for his first win.

The 1980 British Lions lost the first Test in South Africa only 26-22 but there are lies, damned lies, and certain rugby scorelines. The Springboks, recognising the Lions' domination up front, swallowed their manly pride, took a leaf out of the 1977 All Black book and moved the ball wide, where the speed of Rob Louw got them to the breakdown ahead of the Lions' heavier loose forwards, and the counter-attacking of new full-back Gysie Pienaar punched holes in their midfield defence. South Africa scored five tries to one, and only the place kicking of Tony Ward (18 points) kept the Lions within range.

In the second Test, they were again outscored on tries (4-2) but would have won if Ollie Campbell hadn't missed a late penalty. Chances of sharing a series their forwards deserved to win were still about 50/50.

They gave the Springbok pack another terrible time of it in the third Test, but yet again the Lions' backs made mistake after mistake: Colin Patterson going it alone when he should have passed, Andy Irvine dropping the ball with the try line open, Campbell again missing the penalty that would have won it at the very end. The worst gaffe of all, the lapse that decided the series, was perpetrated with only eight minutes left.

South Africa were trailing 10-6 when fly-half Naas Botha kicked towards the Lions' 25. As the ball bumbled along the ground, Clive Woodward trotted after it, then helped it over the line with just a nudge of the boot.

Several things here. First of all, the Lions had stopped bothering to guard against the possibility of a quick throw-in (the ball boys invariably offered a new ball for every line-out, and a quick throw can only be taken if the ball's been retrieved by a player – see OH, REF). Secondly, Woodward, an elegant sidestepping centre who'd made a big impression in England's Grand Slam team, was being played out of position on the right. An experienced international winger would have thumped the ball into the crowd. Woodward, once he'd tapped it into touch, turned away.

Behind him, South African presence of mind was taking advantage of his absence. Left winger Gerrie Germishuys ran after the ball, threw it in to flanker Theuns Stofberg, took the return, and put it down for the equalising try. Botha's superb touchline conversion won the match, and the Lions' success in the last of the series was no more than a well-deserved sop. Woodward didn't play in another Test.

Eric Bristow was lucky to be in the 1983 world professional final. In the first round, Peter Masson had a dart for the match but missed double top and hasn't been heard of since. In the second, Bristow struggled against Dave Lee.

Meanwhile, a fresh-faced 22-year-old 66-1 shot was raising eyebrows by beating the American No. 7 seed Nicky Virachkul in the first round, No. 2 seed John Lowe in the quarter-final and Jocky Wilson in the semi. The Keith Deller Show.

And how. In the final, he led 2-0 and 5-3, then had seven darts to win the title 6-3. He missed them all, Bristow levelled at 5-5 then led 1-0 in the decider, the first time he'd been ahead in the match.

Deller came back to lead 2-1, a single leg from winning the match. Bristow, 121 short of drawing level, threw a single 20 and a cool-under-pressure treble 17 which left him needing the bull.

If he'd gone for it and missed, the worst he would have left himself was 25 with three darts left. If he'd got it, of course, he'd be back to 2-2 with everything to play for.

Bristow threw single 18 to leave himself his favourite double, 16 – but giving Deller the chance to throw 138 for the championship.

Perhaps he thought those seven missed darts would prey on

Above: 'Look, son, it's easy. Treble 20, treble 18, double 12. But remember: I'm still No. 1, alright?' (Colorsport)

the novice's mind. But Deller had made a 121 check-out to win the second leg of the decider, so it should have been obvious that his nerve was holding – and this was a player having the week of his life, liable to hit anything he went for. Reckless, Eric.

Deller – are we surprised? – hit treble 20, treble 18, double 12 to win the title. Bristow, typically, came back to win the next three (7-1, 6-2, 6-0 in the final) after predicting that the young champion wouldn't reach the quarter-final. He was right. Deller lost in the first round. 'He's got no chance in future,' quoth the Cockney. Right again.

After fighting for the British heavyweight title in 1978 and 1981, Billy Aird went on to become a trainer – but the old instincts died hard. It's said that in between rounds of a close fight, he took out his boxer's mouthguard, checked it, cleaned it – and put it in his own mouth.

When four East Germans finished in the top six of the 10 km individual biathlon (skiing and shooting) at the 1988 Winter Olympics, they were naturally expected to win the team event without difficulty. Unfortunately, lead-off man Jürgen Wirth had been testing his rifle in blustery conditions – and forgot to adjust its sights when the wind dropped.

Each miss adds an extra 150 metres to the distance a biathlete has to ski. Wirth missed three of his first five shots, and the extra 450 metres left East Germany a long way back in 12th place. Although Frank-Peter Rötsch (the individual gold medallist), Matthias Jacob and André Sehmisch gave it everything, they finished only fifth.

Adrian Moorhouse won almost everything there was to win at the breaststroke. Olympic gold, four European titles, three Commonwealth, three long-course (i.e. proper) world records.

There wouldn't be any 'almost' but for the 100m final in the 1986 world championships. A European record (fastest time in the heats) had set Moorhouse up as favourite, ahead of even Victor Davis of Canada, the Olympic and Commonwealth champion.

At last swimming like a man who believed he could win at the highest level, Moorhouse beat Davis easily, taking 0.27 off the record he'd set in the heats – then was disqualified.

At the turn, he'd lost concentration and put in an illegal dolphin kick, probably for the first time in years. Davis was given the title and completed the double by winning the 200 in world record time.

In the next world championships, his last chance, Moorhouse finished second, only 0.13 behind Norbert Rozsa of Hungary, who broke his world record by 0.04.

SECONDS OUT

The Long Count (Dempsey v Tunney 1927)

The roaring Twenties, traditionally the golden age of American sport, produced a champion who dominated each one: Babe Ruth baseball, Bobby Jones golf, Red Grange gridiron, Bill Tilden tennis, Johnny Weissmuller swimming, and a non-American, Paavo Nurmi, the track.

In boxing, although there were better boxers among the lower weights – Tiger Flowers, Benny Leonard, Tony Canzoneri – they were mere pygmies in the shadow of the slugger who bestrode the age. This was Dempsey's decade.

For a man who never weighed more than thirteensomething, William Harrison ('Jack') Dempsey's punching power was terrible to behold. The bigger they were, the harder they took it. To win the title, he knocked Jess Willard down seven times in the first round, doing dreadful things to his face and insides. Luis Angel Firpo went the same way nine times in less than two rounds. Phew. Only one question: how (and for godsake why) did they get up so often?

Actually, there were questions aplenty. Dempsey was never a popular champion. Each of his title fights was flawed in some way or other. Willard had outweighed him by more than four stone, but was 37, hadn't fought for three years, and had never enjoyed it when he did. Firpo, big but spectacularly crude, had knocked Dempsey down twice, and if ringside photographers hadn't helped the champion back in he wouldn't have beaten the count. Billy Miske was ill, Georges Carpentier barely a light-heavyweight, Bill Brennan barely a contender. Another average fighter, Tommy Gibbons, lasted 15 rounds. The leading black heavyweight Harry Wills was avoided like the plague. Then there was the question of Dempsey's absence from active duty in the First World War (he was tried as a 'slacker' in 1920). Some, probably the majority, couldn't wait for a new champion.

In 1926 they got one, and didn't like him either. Dempsey, champion for seven years, hadn't defended the title for three, which left him ring rusty and sluggish when he met Gene Tunney in Philadelphia. At first, some thought that a fight held over only ten rounds would suit Tunney's running style, but it was soon clear that ten were more than enough for the 31-year-old champion, who was barely standing at the end, jabbed to a standstill.

Tunney was an ex-marine, which gave the fight an edge and should have made him popular. But if American crowds didn't take to slackers, they did like fighting men, which Dempsey had been in abundance and Tunney, with his defensive style and disdain for the 'sport', wasn't really. In the last round, harmless but throwing punches to the end, Dempsey heard the crowd chant his name for the first time. He was given a standing ovation when he left the ring, and a return fight was a natural.

To earn it, Dempsey had to beat another Jack, Sharkey, who was to win the title in 1932. This he accomplished by the time-honoured expedient of putting in a low blow, waiting for Sharkey to complain to the referee, then throwing a knockout hook. Soldier's Field in Chicago was packed (104,943) for the Tunney rematch.

It went exactly the same way. Tunney was an infinitely better boxer, at least under Queensberry Rules. By the second round, Dempsey was already leaning on the ropes, by the fourth cut and bleeding, at the end unable to see out of one eye, an utter loser on points. For the first six and last three rounds, he was humiliatingly outclassed. But the seventh, now – that was different. That was Dempsey, that was. In every way.

Tunney began the round with a right to the head and the usual flurry of jabs. Dempsey, increasingly desperate, threw a right, then a left hook, then two more punches that didn't matter: the left had done its job. Tunney, on his back near the corner, reaching up for the middle rope, was seconds away from losing the title.

Unfortunately for Jack, there were more seconds than usual, they cost him the fight, and they were his own fault. Before the bout, he'd been warned that in the event of a knockdown the boxer who'd done the knocking down had to retire to a neutral corner before the referee could start counting. Dempsey, brought up under the old prizefighting rules, was accustomed to standing over an opponent until he got up. He did that here. When referee Dave Barry reached the count of five, he realised Dempsey was too close, stopped the count, sent Dempsey back to the corner, and restarted from scratch. When he reached nine, Tunney got up.

Estimates vary, but it's likely that the famous Long Count lasted 14 seconds, just enough for Tunney to regather his faculties, use them to keep Dempsey at bay for the rest of the round, knock him down in the next, win easily, and retire as undefeated champion the following year.

Dempsey, whose blunder had cost him the chance to become the first heavyweight to regain the world title, fought a good many exhibitions but effectively retired, immeasurably popular in defeat, to run a world-famous restaurant in New York. If the service sometimes took a few seconds longer, it was probably worth the wait.

Below: Go and stand in the corner till you get it right. Dempsey counts his chickens, Tunney his lucky stars (Syndication International)

LOOK, NO HANDS

dropped balls and batons

In 1940, the great George Halas and his assistant at Chicago, Clark Shaughnessy, effectively invented modern American football by resurrecting the ancient T formation in which the quarterback was the pivot of the attack. Still the universal method now, it paid off immediately at the time.

If Halas and the Bears had the ideal quarterback for the T in Sid Luckman, their opponents in the 1940 championship game, the Washington Redskins, had perhaps the greatest thrower of all time, Slingin' Sammy Baugh. It's said that when he arrived from Texas, the Redskins' coach told him that he had to be able to hit the receiver in the eye with every pass. 'Which eye?' said Sam. At the end of his first pro season, he'd thrown three touchdown passes to beat the Bears in the 1937 championship game.

Three years later, after the Bears had taken an early 7-0 lead, Washington reached the Chicago 26-yard line and Sammy stepped back to sling. His pass picked out wide receiver Charlie Malone unmarked in the end zone, Malone caught the ball, hugged it to his chest – and dropped it.

Instead of drawing level, the Redskins went on to lose 73-0 (no misprint), not only the heaviest defeat in any championship game but in all NFL history.

In the first round of the sprint relay at the 1936 Olympics, the German quartet set a world record that lasted 16 years but shouldn't have survived 24 hours.

In the final the following day, they were nine yards clear at the last changeover when Marie Dollinger handed the baton to Ilse Dörffeldt, who fiddled, fumbled, and dropped. Their disqualification handed the gold medal to the USA.

Twenty-four years later, Dollinger's daughter Brunhilde Hendrix won a silver medal in West Germany's sprint relay team.

History repeated itself in 1948. The Australian team broke Germany's world record in the first round and were leading in the final when Winsome Cripps made the last pass to Marjorie Jackson, the fastest woman of her day, who'd won the sprint double earlier in the Games. Jackson's hand hit Cripps' knee and the baton was knocked loose. She picked it up and ran on, but

Australia finished fifth and 15-year-old Barbara Jones became the youngest ever Olympic athletics gold medallist thanks to the USA's second lightning strike.

In 1961 and 1962, the famous quarterback YA Tittle was on the losing side in the NFL championship game against the Green Bay Packers. In 1963, against the Chicago Bears, he seemed to be third time lucky. His touchdown pass to Frank Gifford had given the New York Giants an early 7-0 lead. On their next play, the Bears fumbled, and Tittle was given the ball on their 31-yard line.

His throw found Del Shofner completely free in the end zone. Shofner's fingers, chilled by the freezing conditions, couldn't hold it. Tittle went on to throw five interceptions, including another pass to Shofner with ten seconds of the game left, the Giants lost 14-10 (their fifth defeat in their last five championship deciders) and Tittle never won an NFL title.

Below: *Dollinger and Dörfeldt, already celebrating the gold, drop the aluminium* (Popperfoto)

Foot in mouth

"St Helens have really got their tails between their teeth."
MALCOLM LORD

In the 1978 rugby league Challenge Cup final, holders Leeds made a bad start against St Helens, their predecessors as cup winners. A high hanging ball close to their line was badly fumbled by full-back Henry Oulton and winger John Atkinson, letting Graham Liptrot in for a try converted by captain Geoff Pimblett. When Bill Francis scored a second converted try, Saints led 10-0.

Then Atkinson and Oulton redeemed themselves: Atkinson, in his 400th game for Leeds, scored a try converted by Oulton. A Pimblett penalty put St Helens 12-5 ahead at half-time, but a dropped goal by David Ward and tries by David Smith and Phil Cookson levelled the scores, after which two more dropped goals, by the talented John Holmes and Ward again, put Leeds 14-12 ahead.

In the last few seconds, Peter Glynn's pass reached centre Derek Noonan, who had a man unmarked outside him, not a Leeds tackler in sight, and the line only a step away. Noonan dropped the ball.

Pimblett had hit a post in the second half, two of Leeds' tries seemed to come from forward passes – and now this. 'The less said about it the better,' said Saints coach Eric Ashton.

St Helens have reached the final another three times, but haven't won the cup since 1976.

Superbowl XIII (1979) was a classic. The two best teams of the decade, two great quarterbacks (Terry Bradshaw and Roger Staubach), a final score of 35-31.

Near the end of the third quarter, the holders, the Dallas Cowboys, were 4 points behind when they reached the Pittsburgh Steelers' 10-yard line, from which Staubach threw to tight end Jackie Smith, unmarked in the end zone.

The previous season, Smith had retired on medical advice, threatened by paralysis from wear and tear in his neck. The Cowboys signed him as back-up. He was 38. He and Staubach were the oldest players in the team. He dropped the pass.

Both teams scored two touchdowns in the fourth quarter, and the Steelers beat the Cowboys by 4 points for the second time in four Superbowls.

Great Britain, back in the rugby league World Cup final for the first time since 1977, gave Australia as good as they got at

Wembley in 1992, leading 6-4 at half-time through three penalty goals by Deryck Fox to two by Mal Meninga.

The lead held till 13 minutes from time when winger Alan Hunte took a pass in his own 25 and ran at the Australian half-back Allan Langer.

He'd done exactly the same thing three times in the match. Each time Langer had tackled him high. This time he went in low, Hunte went head over heels, and lost the ball.

With Langer caught in the tackle, acting half-back Steve Walters threw out a long pass to his younger brother Kevin, who'd come on as a substitute and now moved the ball on to the distinctive scrum-capped figure of Steve Renouf, a centre winning his first cap.

Renouf, running straight, broke substitute John Devereux's tackle and went over in the corner for the only try of the match. Meninga's fine conversion put Australia 10-6 ahead.

There was still time for a comeback, but Britain hadn't looked like scoring a try (Australia's coach Bob Fulton said they 'never made a break at all') and the rest was anti-climax. Tough on Alan 'obviously I'm gutted' Hunte.

Australia had won yet another world final against the hosts in England (hockey 1986, rugby union 1991), Great Britain haven't won the rugby league World Cup since 1972.

When they took a 15-12 lead against Wales in 1985, it looked as if England were at last going to win a rugby international in Cardiff for the first time in 22 years. Then Welsh fly-half Jonathan Davies, winning his first cap, hoisted a high kick to the English line, where full-back Chris Martin dropped it, reached for it on the ground, couldn't get there, and saw Davies score the try. England lost 24-15 and had to wait till 1991 for that Cardiff success. Martin wasn't capped again.

Eighteen-year-old rower Vyacheslav Ivanov was so pleased with his Olympic gold medal for the 1956 single sculls that he threw it high in the air on the rostrum – and dropped it in Melbourne's Lake Wendouree. He dived after it but had no luck. Frogmen went in: nothing. Later he was presented with a replacement. He won (and held on to) the gold again in 1960 and 1964.

CATCHES LOSE MATCHES

(missed stumpings don't help)

Clive Hubert Lloyd scored 7515 runs in Test cricket, quite a few courtesy of Indian hospitality.

In his very first Test, at Bombay in December 1966, India scored 296 in the first innings of the series, then reduced the West Indies to 82-3 despite dropping a catch off Conrad Hunte. Lloyd, bamboozled like everyone else by Chandrasekhar's leg-spin, had reached only 8 in his first Test innings when he gave a simple slip chance to Ajit Wadekar, the other new cap, who put it down. Lloyd made 82, Hunte 101, the West Indies 421. They won the Test, and the series 2-0.

Big Clive was made captain for the first time before the 1974–75 series against India. In the decisive fifth Test, again in Bombay, Lloyd scored 242 not out after being dropped when he'd made 8, 70 and 154. West Indies won the series 3-2.

Two down after the third Test of the 1983–84 series, India made 463 in the fourth and had chances to take a big first innings lead – but Viv Richards was dropped twice on his way to 120, and Lloyd and Jeff Dujon added 119 while being dropped five times between them. Altogether the Indians put down nine chances in the total of 393. Set 243 in the second innings, West Indies were 68-4 but escaped to force the draw and win the series. Hubert probably knew it was going to turn out right all along: this was Bombay again, after all.

He had friends in Australia too. When they'd held West Indies to 50-3 in the first World Cup final (1975), he came in and changed everything with 102 off 82 balls, but only after giving an early chance to Ross Edwards, one of the great cover fielders. Australia lost by 17 runs.

At Adelaide in the third and final Test of the 1981–82 series, Lloyd made 77 not out in the second innings – after the Australians had dropped him three times and Faoud Bacchus once. West Indies won by 5 wickets and escaped with a 1-1 draw. Allan Border, who top-scored in each innings (78 and 126), never played in a team that won a series against them.

Foot in mouth
"Well, I'll remember that catch for many a dying day."
BRIAN JOHNSTON

Dropping catches that cost entire series is almost as old as Test cricket itself. Back in 1884, in the first Test ever played at Lord's,

Allan C Steel made his famous 148 against Australia after being dropped at short leg on 48. England won the match by an innings and the series 1-0.

The ageless Wilfred Rhodes shared in an opening stand of 323 with Jack Hobbs against Australia in 1912 as well as taking more first-class wickets than anyone else, 127 of them in Test cricket. Fifteen of those were taken in Melbourne during the second match of the 1903–04 series (7-56 and 8-68). Who knows how many he might have picked up if eight catches hadn't been dropped off his bowling! England won by 185 runs and took the series 3-2.

England won the first Test of the 1909 Ashes series by 10 wickets then made 269 in the first innings of the second. Australia's reply was founded on left-hander Vernon Ransford's 143, his only Test century.

He should never have been allowed to reach it. The England captain Archie MacLaren put him down at slip, Dick Lilley at the wicket. On 61, he was dropped at slip again. England lost by 9 wickets and set Australia on the way to winning the series 2-1.

At Headingley in 1948, Norman Yardley declared to set Australia 404 to win and make certain of retaining the Ashes. No team had ever scored 400 to win a Test match.

A second-wicket partnership of 301 between Arthur Morris (182) and Don Bradman (173) settled things – after England had dropped *eight* catches. Bradman, on 59, gave a chance to Yardley himself; on 108 a stumping chance to Godfrey Evans. When he'd scored only 22, he was put down by Jack Crapp. That said it all.

Morris was dropped twice, Australia made their 404 for the loss of only 3 wickets, and won the series 4-0.

England, usually so well prepared under Ray Illingworth, went into the first Test of the 1972 Ashes series without a single

Willie Watson was a ball-winning half-back at soccer who won four England caps from 1949 to 1950, and a patient left-handed batsman who played in 23 Tests from 1951 to 1959. In his first against Australia, the second of the 1953 series, he came in on the fourth evening of the second Test when England, needing 343 to win, were 12-3. In the last over of the day, bowled by leg-spinner Doug Ring, he gave two chances to fast bowler Ray Lindwall at short leg: Lindwall missed the first and went the wrong way for the other!

Watson stayed throughout most of the final day, making 109 and sharing a five-hour partnership of 163 with Trevor Bailey that saved the match. England won the last Test to take the series 1-0 and regain the Ashes after a record gap of almost exactly 19 years.

Foot in mouth

"If Gower had stopped that, it would have decapitated his hand."
FAROUKH ENGINEER

recognised slip fielder. Tony Greig, who sometimes fielded there for Sussex, was pressed into service – but after that Illingworth had to ask for a show of hands.

For some reason (probably a desire to escape the longueurs of the deep) John Snow, of all people, volunteered – then proceeded to catch everything in practice. He lined up alongside Greig and Illingworth in Australia's first innings.

The score had reached 14-0 on the kind of damp, chilly Old Trafford morning to warm any medium-pacer's cockles. Geoff Arnold was one of the best of the species, a big swinger of the ball. One of them found the edge of Keith Stackpole's bat and shot head-high to Snow, who went up in a flurry of arms and hair and got a hand to the ball, but only enough to send it down to third man for four.

Next ball, Stackpole edged again, this time at a nice comfortable height to Greig, who was to become one of the great slip fielders: an incredible 87 catches in 58 Tests. He had it under control, then lost it.

Back went Arnold, down came the next ball, across came the edge of the bat. Snow, more upright after that first chance, was hit on the boot. A furious Illingworth banished him to the outfield where most of his poetry had been conceived. Three dropped catches off as many balls seems to be a Test record.

Greig later dropped Bruce Francis off D'Oliveira, then Illingworth himself was hit in the chest at slip (and went on television to say that Old Trafford was the worst ground in the country for sighting the ball!).

None of this affected the result – Australia mustered only 142 and lost by 89 runs – but if those three successive chances had stuck, Arnold (and not Peter Loader in 1957) would be the last English bowler to take a Test hat-trick.

Back in 1938, another dropped catch had cost an England bowler a hat-trick. At Lord's, the great pace of 6ft 5in bowler Ken Farnes bowled Bill O'Reilly then had Ernie McCormick caught by Charlie Barnett. The third ball, which would have wrapped up the Australian innings, went through Leslie O'Brien Fleetwood-Smith before you could say his name, took the edge – and was dropped by Denis Compton at slip. The match was drawn.

By 1973, New Zealand had been playing England for more than 43 years without winning a single Test. In the 44th (year and match) between the two countries, at Lord's in 1973, they scored what was then their highest total in Test cricket, 551-9 dec, and still had two hours to bowl England out for the second time when medium-pacer Geoff Arnold came to the wicket.

England were only 70 ahead with two wickets left. The first ball Arnold faced, from off-spinning all-rounder Vic Pollard, seemed to get a very thin edge: Ken Wadsworth, a likeable and talented wicketkeeper, dropped it. Next ball, another edge, this time a definite one: again Wadsworth put it down. Arnold batted for 90 minutes to eke out the draw, England won the series 2-0.

New Zealand had to wait more than four years for that first win over England (in the 48th match against them) but Ken Wadsworth wasn't there to share in it. He died in 1976, aged 29, after making 96 dismissals in Test cricket.

Making his Test comeback after more than three years, Geoff Boycott began badly at Trent Bridge in 1977. At one stage, replying to Australia's 243, England were 82-5 and Boycott had run out local favourite Derek Randall. No surprise there. He scored his first boundary off the 115th ball he received. Ditto.

He'd made a slow, strangled 20 when Len Pascoe found the edge of his bat and gave Rick McCosker a comfortable chance at slip. He put it down. If he'd hung on, England would have been 87-6. It was the crucial miss of the series.

Boycott made 107, sharing a record-equalling stand of 215 with Alan Knott, and (he must have liked this) becoming only the second player to bat on every day of a five-day Test. In the next, at Headingley, he made 191 (the famous 100th hundred), and averaged 147.33 in the series, which England won 3-0 to regain the Ashes.

Needing to win their last match of 1977 to be sure of becoming county champions for the first time in a century, Gloucestershire set Hampshire a second innings target of 271.

Hants, with no stake in the outcome, threw the bat. In the last over before lunch, Gordon Greenidge lashed out at spinner David Graveney and gave a chance to Brian Brain, a useful medium-fast bowler whose parents thought they had a sense of humour. He dropped it.

Greenidge, then on 30, made 94 at a run a minute. David Turner, dropped when he'd made 8, scored 28. Hampshire won by 6 wickets, Kent and Middlesex shared the championship, and Gloucester still haven't won it since 1877.

In 1984, half an hour into the last day of the second Test, David Gower declared and set the West Indies 342 to win. It seems to

After Glamorgan had made only 177 on a damp outfield in the 1977 Gillette Cup final, Middlesex began their reply by losing their captain Mike Brearley to the first ball of the innings. Soon afterwards, Clive Radley had made only 2 when he edged a ball from Malcolm Nash (of Sobers' six sixes fame) to second slip, where the West Indies Test all-rounder Collis King dropped it. Radley went on to make 85 and be made man of the match as Middlesex won by 5 wickets. Glamorgan didn't win a one-day title till 1993.

Essex, who'd never won the NatWest Trophy (ex-Gillette Cup), made 280 in the 1985 final against Notts after Ken McEwan was dropped by Chris Broad off Kevin Saxelby when he'd made 16. He scored 46 not out and Essex won by one run.

Two years later, Notts won it for the first time by beating Northants by 3 wickets – after Richard Hadlee had been dropped three times (once by Allan Lamb off a stroke that went for six) on his way to 70 not out and the man of the match award.

Two years after that (1989), it was Essex's turn to help Notts to a major one-day trophy, the Benson & Hedges: they dropped Derek Randall on 37 and 39 and lost the final by 3 wickets off the very last ball.

have been a decision he'd slept on (his batsmen had accepted the umpire's offer of the light when there were still 53 minutes left on the fourth evening) but England nevertheless had 5½ hours in which to bowl the West Indies out and square the series.

It soon became clear that they weren't going to win it, and the last chance of a draw disappeared when Greenidge had scored 110.

Botham's gone, and he'll be missed, there'll never be another, etc – but lest we forget: against the West Indies he averaged 35.18 with the ball and only 21.40 with the bat. Still, there's no doubt about his slip catching (120 in 102 Tests): when Greenidge edged Bob Willis to him, he'd have expected to hold it.

Not this time. Greenidge made 214 not out (his first Test double century), West Indies won by 9 wickets with virtually six overs to spare and went on to their first blackwash against England, Greenidge making 223 at Old Trafford.

In the fifth Test against the West Indies in 1991, Botham hit the winning runs to give England a share of the series. It was his last innings against them and the only time they didn't get him out. He scored 4.

Whereas England had always looked likely to reach the 1992 World Cup final, Pakistan had staggered in, losing their first match by 10 wickets, winning only one of the first five, squeaking into the semi-finals when the West Indies self-destructed. Above all, they were saved by rain after England had bowled them out for 74.

So they were natural underdogs in Melbourne, especially when they reached only 34-2 (including 18 extras) off the first 17 overs with Javed Miandad and his captain Imran Khan making just 4 runs off 63 balls. England's policy of packing the team with all-rounders (Botham, Chris Lewis, Dermot Reeve) seemed to be paying off.

Imran, in contrast, believed in specialists in all types of cricket. Dig in against England's medium-pacers, he argued, and they won't have the speed or spin to get you out when the slogging starts.

He was proved right, eventually. Pakistan scored only 49 from their first 20 overs but 200 from the last 30, setting England a rate of exactly 5 an over to win. Bowled out by specialists like Wasim Akram, Aqib Javed and Mushtaq Ahmed, they fell 22 runs short. In the end it hadn't even been close.

But the match had turned on a single dropped catch. When he'd scored only 9, Imran top-edged the ball to Graham Gooch, who didn't have far to move, got hands to it – and crash. One captain went on to make 72 in his last match for Pakistan, the other became the only player to finish on the losing side in three World Cup finals. The chance won't come again.

After making only 208 in the 1992 NatWest final, Leicestershire needed a quick wicket or two when Northants batted. Instead, they posted just a single slip.

Justin Benson dropped Alan Fordham when he'd made 18 and Rob Bailey when he'd scored only 2. Fordham scored 91 and was made man of the match, Bailey 72. They put on 144 in 35 overs and Northants won by 8 wickets.

It wasn't Benson's day. He'd made a duck in Leicestershire's innings.

Above: *Blatant tampering with the stumps. Imran and the boys give thanks for Gooch's generosity in the World Cup final* (Popperfoto)

In 1993 New Zealand reached the women's World Cup final for the first time by beating the hot favourites Australia and not allowing any of their opponents to total more than 112. England, in the round-robin match, had managed only 99.

In the final, they almost doubled that – but they had help. Wendy Watson was dropped twice before being bowled for 5. Much more importantly, Carole Hodges was put down on 29 and Jo Chamberlain on 7. Hodges made 45, Chamberlain a hard-hitting 38, England 195-5 to win the World Cup for the first time in twenty years.

PASSING THE PARCEL

In the first international of their 1924–25 tour, the All Blacks had their work cut out against a strong Irish team (the Hewitt brothers, the Stephenson brothers, witty and dirty Jammie Clinch) which held them to 0-0 at half-time.

Seven minutes into the second half, the Irish captain Harry Stephenson, a good winger who lived in the shadow of his brother George, picked up a loose ball under his own posts, then made the mistake of running instead of kicking. Worse still, when the great Bert Cooke's tackle came in, he threw out a pass instead of holding on and giving his forwards time to get there.

Fred Lucas picked the ball up and gave it to right wing 'Snowy' Svenson, who ran in for the try. Three minutes later, Mark Nicholls' penalty doubled the lead.

Poor Harry had a chance to redeem himself late on, but was pushed into touch after taking George's pass. The All Blacks held on to win 6-0 and won the other four internationals as well, indeed all 30 matches on tour. They've never lost to Ireland.

Late in the third quarter of the 1948 championship game, Chicago Cardinals quarterback Ray Mallouf tried to hand the ball off to Elmer Angsman but got his angles wrong and missed him.

Kilroy was there. The Philadelphia Eagles lineman Bucko Kilroy picked the ball up, Bosh Pritchard made six yards on the subsequent play, and the Eagles moved the ball on for the eventual touchdown, the only score of the game.

In the equivalent fixture five years later, the Cleveland Browns quarterback Otto Graham had the worst game of his professional career, completing only two out of 15 passes for a miserable total of 20 yards. When he lost the ball in a sack by the Detroit Lions' Les Bingaman (who weighed 22 stone), the Lions scored the first touchdown of the game.

At the end of the game, with Cleveland 17-16 down, Graham threw long towards Dante Lavelli. The pass wasn't good enough, the play too ambitious with more than two minutes left. The ball was picked off by Carl Karilivacz and the Lions beat the Browns in the championship decider for the second consecutive year.

The Browns (who at last beat the Lions in the big game the following year) played in six consecutive championship games 1950–55, winning only the last two.

In the last minute of the 1938 rugby league Challenge Cup final, the score 4-4, Barrow's captain Alec Troup threw out a pass that went to ground, where it was picked up by opposing centre Albert Gear, who scored the only try of the match to give Salford the Cup for the only time in their history.

At Murrayfield in 1955, Wales were only 9-8 down in the closing minutes when scrum-half Rex Willis threw out a horrible pass near his own line: it missed fly-half Cliff Morgan completely (see PICK OF THE WEAK) and Scotland's new scrum-half JA Nichol scored the try that settled it. An important 'it' too: Scotland's first win since beating Wales in 1951, ending a record run of 17 successive defeats, including a 44-0 humiliation (worth 62-0 now) by South Africa.

After the 1971 Five Nations championship, an extra match was arranged at Murrayfield 100 years to the day after the very first international. It didn't take long to make itself a memorable anniversary.

Jock Turner kicked off for Scotland, Bob Hiller caught the ball near his corner flag and passed inside to Jeremy Janion, who should have kicked for touch but instead handed the hot potato to Dick Cowman, who scooped it back to his captain John Spencer, who couldn't hold it. The big Scottish centre John Frame fell on the ball for one of the fastest tries in international rugby: 12 seconds max.

Scotland scored another four tries and won the match 26-6. They'd also won in 1871.

The 1977 British Lion forwards carried on where they'd left off in South Africa in 1974, outplaying their opponents in the tight to such an extent that the All Blacks were reduced to taking three-man scrums in the fourth Test, a shamefaced climbdown for a country that had always prided itself on the strength of its pack.

Despite this, the Lions went into that last Test needing a win to square the series. Several reasons for this. First of all, New Zealand had bitten the bullet, admitting that their front five weren't as good as Price, Wheeler, Cotton, Brown & Co, and had gone for pace in the back row (bringing in Graham Mourie) and a passing scrum-half (Lyn Davis) in place of national icon Syd Going.

More importantly, the Lions had picked some desperately mediocre backs. The standard of British threequarter play had been in decline for years, but even so, even with so many irreplaceable players making themselves unavailable (Gareth Edwards, Gerald Davies, JPR Williams), some of the choices were

Leeds were leading 6-2 in the 1957 Challenge Cup final when Barrow's Jack Grundy (man of the match in the 1955 final) passed the ball to Leeds forward Don Robinson near his own line. Robinson went over for the try, Leeds won only 9-7.

The 1972 final was Leeds' turn to be on the receiving end (as it were): their hooker Tony Fisher threw the ball back, it went to ground, St Helens loose forward Graham Rees turned it into a try converted by man of the match Kel Coslett. Only 35 seconds had gone: the fastest Challenge Cup try at Wembley. Leeds lost in the final for the second successive year.

bizarre. Although Wales had won the Triple Crown, their record quota of 16 players in the 30 was preposterously high: the likes of David Burcher, Gareth Evans and Elgan Rees were very lucky to become British Lions.

The biggest loss, that of Mervyn Davies through injury, led to Phil Bennett being made captain of Wales and of the Lions on the tour. He admitted he wasn't up to it, but it didn't help that the two scrum-halves inside him, Doug Morgan and the uncapped Brynmor Williams, weren't as good as *anyone* in the New Zealand provinces.

Even with all these self-imposed burdens, the Lions led 9-3 in the last Test and the control of their forwards was total. Then Morgan missed an easy penalty and Bevan Wilson kicked one to bring the All Blacks up to within three points. With only four minutes left, their fly-half Doug Bruce put up a high ball which Gareth Evans dropped, leaving Bennett to scurry back with his mop and bucket.

The Lions captain, who didn't trust himself to kick with his left foot, hooked a difficult kick over his shoulder with his right. All he had to do was find touch, leaving his forwards to dominate yet another line-out. Instead, he put in his last poor kick of an unhappy tour, missed touch, and saw Bill Osborne catch the ball and pump it back upfield.

Lions centre Steve Fenwick caught it, had a chance to kick clear, but passed it on to Peter Wheeler. Wrong move. Wheeler, who wasn't expecting a pass in that position, couldn't hold it, and the ball bounced up neatly into the hands of All Black No. 8 Lawrie Knight, who went over in the corner. The Lions lost 10-9 and didn't win another series for twelve years.

In the last minute, the ball had gone out to Andy Irvine, who lost it. A recent All Black coach, John J Stewart, caught the mood: as soon as the ball reached the Lions' backs, he said, New Zealand were out of danger. 'I knew they'd make a cock of it.'

Those twelve years later, the Lions were on the other end of an unexpected pass that decided a Test series.

After losing the first international in Australia 30-12, they came from behind to win the second 19-12. During the third, at the Sydney Football Stadium, fly-half Rob Andrew missed with a drop at goal, the ball wandering off into Australia's left-hand corner. Ieuan Evans set off not so much in pursuit but because wingers are expected to chase this kind of thing.

Evans had played in seven matches on the tour, scoring only one try. Ahead of him, his opposite number picked the ball up with time to spare.

David Campese's had one of the most successful careers in international rugby. World Cup winner in 1991, scorer of a world record number of Test tries (57 at the time this was written, and

Foot in mouth
"Mind you, 39 is a nice round number."
CLIFF MORGAN

Left: *The buck usually stops here. Campo's used it to score a record number of international tries.*
(Allsport/Shaun Botterill)

unlikely to stop there). Much of the success has been at the expense of British teams: three tries against Wales, five against England, six each against Scotland and Ireland.

So we can be forgiven a little glee. Defensively, they say Campo's not so hot – and if the evidence isn't always forthcoming, it came forth mob-handed here. In the previous Test, his two dropped garryowens in succession had presented the Lions with their second try. Here he picked up Andrew's kick and decided to run from his own line instead of kicking to touch.

Then, when he saw Evans coming in, he threw a horribly sudden pass at full-back Greg Martin, who was forgiven for dropping it. Evans dived in to score the Lions' only try of the match, which they won by a single point to become the first British Isles team for 90 years to win a series after losing the opening match.

Later in the match, Campese stamped on David Sole's face. Probably pure frustration at not practising what he preached to children: 'I always tell them never to throw a pass in defence without knowing exactly where you're passing it.'

Four years later, on the same Sydney pitch, Australia were leading 9-0 when the Springbok full-back Heinrich Fuls put in a grubber kick towards their line. Campo, going back, fumbled it, Pieter Muller picked it up and went over. South Africa led 14-9 at half-time and won 19-12, their most important win since they returned to international rugby.

THROWING WOBBLIES

bad throws

In the 1945 American football championship decider, the great Sammy Baugh (see LOOK, NO HANDS) was back leading the Redskins against the Cleveland Rams. In the first quarter, under pressure on his own line, Baugh stepped back into the end zone and unleashed the golden arm.

No-one ever found a more original way to lose a title. His throw hit the back of his own post and landed in the end zone, giving away a safety for the first two points of the game. Washington lost by one, 15-14. It was Slingin' Sam's last appearance in a championship game.

In the 1969 Superbowl, Joe Namath's Match, the Baltimore Colts were huge favourites but trailed 7-0 with 25 seconds left in the second quarter. On the New York Jets' 42-yard line, Baltimore quarterback Earl Morrall handed off to running back Tom Matte, who shot up the right then abruptly stopped and gave Morrall a return pass: the classic old flea-flicker play.

Morrall needed only to find wide receiver Jimmy Orr, completely unguarded on the Jets' 10-yard line, to tie the score. Instead, despite having used the flea-flicker against Atlanta during the regular season, he went for Jerry Hill on the 12-yard line. Jim Hudson intercepted, the Colts trailed 7-0 at half-time, Morrall was substituted after completing only 6 out of 17 passes, Namath & Co won 16-7, and the Colts had to wait two more years before winning their first Superbowl, by which time neither Morrall nor Orr were in the team.

Foot in mouth

"There are two ways of getting the ball. One way is from your own players, and that's the only way."
TERRY VENABLES

Few paid any attention to the big blond Finn at the start of the javelin run-up in the 1987 world championships. He'd finished 17th at the Europeans a year earlier, and his best throw of the new season was several metres short of consideration.

He lived down to all that now. As he reached the end of his run, he put in the customary hitch kick to get one leg behind the other as a fulcrum, got his wires and legs crossed, tripped, and speared the ground *behind* the line. Brilliant.

No-one enjoying the moment on television would have believed for one moment that they were looking at the world champion elect. His last throw in the final won him the title by a metre.

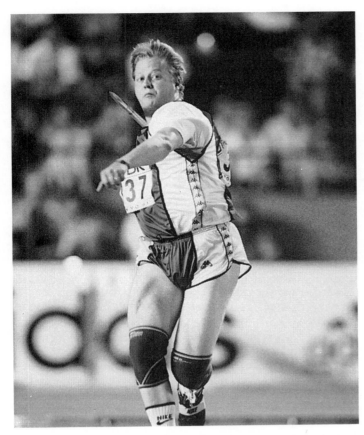

Left: *Seppo Raty has another stab at the world title*
(Allsport/Gray Mortimore)

This was the start of big things for Seppo Raty – second place in the next world championships, Olympic silver and bronze, two world records in 1991 – but none of them vivid enough to overshadow that unique achievement: the only champion to throw the javelin minus 10cm!

In the 1992 world professional championship, Mike Gregory matched No. 1 seed Phil Taylor almost dart for dart. Taylor threw 27 180s during the competition, Gregory 26. Taylor hit seven check-outs of 100 or more, Gregory six.

The final was as close as it could have been. Both threw 11 maximums to take the match into a deciding game. In the sixth leg, Gregory had two shots at double 8; in the tenth, two darts at double top and two more at double 10. Six times within a single shot of becoming world champion, he missed them all.

Taylor won 6-5 to regain the title he'd won in 1990. For Gregory, winner of major events for a number of years, it may have been his best shot at the really big one.

Irish record holder Declan Hegarty didn't qualify for the final of the 1983 world championships or 1984 Olympics – but impressed the TV millions with one special throw. Somewhere among his three rotations, he lost count and control, threw his implement in the wrong direction – and demolished the hammer cage.

ZOO KEEPERS

goalies: a breed apart

Bob Wilson said it (or at least the title of his book did): You've Got To Be Crazy. *And the man who let Steve Heighway's shot in at the near post in the 1971 FA Cup final should know. Arsenal, of course, won that match to complete the Double, so it didn't count. Other custodial lapses were more repercussive . . .*

After 19 minutes of the 1898 FA Cup final, Derby County 'keeper Jack Fryer was unsighted when Arthur 'Sailor' Capes put Nottingham Forest ahead. The great Steve Bloomer equalised, but big Jack's troubles were anything but over.

Two minutes from half-time, Forest outside-right Tom McInnes beat a man and found England international Charlie Richards, who shot straight at the keeper.

Fryer, who'd already 'frustrated several well-intentioned shots', clutched the ball to his midriff, held it for a second, then spilled it, virtually threw it at the feet of Capes, who couldn't miss. John McPherson made it 3-1 in the second-half – but that second goal 'undoubtedly cost County the game.'

No-one had a more terrible time in FA Cup finals than John Spencer Fryer, 'Derby's lengthy custodian'. The following year he conceded four against Sheffield United; in 1903 he was injured as Derby lost by a record 6-0 to Bury. He never won a winner's medal, Derby didn't win the cup till 1946.

The most famous goalkeeping error in any FA Cup final was made in 1927, by a Welshman playing against a Welsh team who had an Irishman in goal.

Arsenal, in their first final, were still three years away from beginning their domination of League football but had five England internationals in the team, including the very fast winger Joe Hulme and the veteran captain and schemer Charlie Buchan, of the long legs and big football brain. Cardiff City, who'd lost 1-0 in the final two years earlier, had no Englishmen at all, but their assortment of Welsh, Scots and Irish included eight internationals. Chances: about even.

The first half was certainly that, and very dull. Two dogged half-back lines cancelled each other out (Welsh international Bob

John was playing for Arsenal) and neither side had a really high-class striker.

As if to prove it, Cardiff's Scottish centre-forward Hugh Ferguson hit a weak ground shot from the edge of the area with 15 minutes left. The ball rolled along slowly enough for Arsenal keeper Dan Lewis to go down on his knees and scoop it up into his midriff.

The story goes that he was wearing a brand new jersey, that the wool was still greasy, that since then Arsenal goalkeepers always wash their shirts before playing in a final. More importantly, Lewis seems to have seen Len Davies running in out of the corner of his eye and taken the rest of it off the ball, which slid under his body and horribly slowly over the line.

It was the only time the FA Cup was won by a club from outside England. By the time Arsenal won it for the first time, three years later, Lewis was in the reserves.

It's called the Matthews Cup Final, so it must have been dominated by a single player, yes? Well, it was certainly decided by a man called Stan . . .

One of them, Mortensen, scored a hat-trick (when he died in 1991, someone said 'I suppose they'll call it the Matthews Funeral') against a team whose tactics were open to question: they left an injured man (Eric Bell) to protect Ralph Banks, increasingly lame himself, from Matthews. But the turning point in the match was the result of a goalkeeping error.

George Farm, Blackpool's Scottish international, had let a 25-yarder by Nat Lofthouse drop out of his arms into the net, then failed to cover another long shot from Bobby Langton which went in off Willie Moir's shoulder.

His skin was saved by his opposite number. Blackpool were 3-1 down and missing chances against a weakened team when Matthews lofted in another cross from the right. Too long, too high – and too easy for Stan Hanson in the Bolton goal. He went up, got his fingers to the ball, let it fall behind him, and was standing up watching when Mortensen stabbed it in before colliding with the far post.

Two more goals in the last three minutes won it 4-3 for Blackpool. One Stan scored the first, another made the winner, the Bolton one never won a winner's medal.

West Auckland Town reached only one FA Amateur Cup final, in 1961, and had real chances to win it, 1) when Walthamstow Avenue's inside-left Don Saggers pulled a ligament in the first

Foot in mouth

"I'd give my right arm to be a concert pianist."
BOBBY ROBSON

Tottenham were dominating the 1963 European Cup-Winners' Cup final when half-time came and changed everything. Almost immediately, holders Atletico Madrid pulled a goal back from the penalty spot and ran riot in the next 20 minutes, missing chances, pulling the Spurs midfield (minus the injured Dave Mackay) left and right. Another goal looked imminent.

It came down from the blue. Terry Dyson hit a cross much too close to the goalkeeper and the near post. It dropped almost vertically, Edgardo Madinabeytia held it in both hands above his head, then let it slip back – almost tossed it behind him – into the net.

Tottenham, 3-1 up, had no more problems. Greaves scored a fourth, Dyson a virtuoso fifth, a British team had won one of the European cups for the first time.

minute and was a passenger thereafter, changing places with Brian Harvey, 2) when winger Alan Douglass meandered inside to put them ahead. If they could hold out for another 12 minutes, a second half against a ten-man team awaited.

The lead lasted three minutes, then the ball came back off a post and Reggie Groves equalised. The score was still 1-1 with just over 20 minutes left when a long ball drifted into the West Auckland penalty area. Goalkeeper Brian Bowmaker went up, all a-quiver, and dropped it in front of Jim Lewis, who knocked in the winner from close range.

The following year, underdogs Hounslow Town reached *their* only Amateur Cup final. When a header from John Fennell beat Crook Town goalkeeper Ray Snowball, Bruce Patterson scored – but it was only the equaliser. To win the cup, Hounslow had really needed to go ahead.

Instead they'd had an early goal disallowed, and seven minutes before Patterson's goal their own 'keeper Peter Rhodes, who'd played well, picked off a bad high cross from Jimmy McMillan – and fumbled it into his own net.

In the replay, Snowball made some good saves, Hounslow missed chances and lost 4-0.

Chesham United rampaged through the 1968 Amateur Cup as 1000-1 outsiders, didn't win one of their 12 matches between semi and final, fell to fourth from bottom of Division 2 in the Athenian League – but should have walked off with the trophy. Even when favourites Leytonstone lost Bobby Hames with a leg injury after only ten minutes and his replacement, 19-year-old John Albon, with a broken leg, Chesham didn't take their chance against ten men.

Twenty minutes from time, their goalkeeper Dennis Wells went up unchallenged for Les Tilley's simple cross, and dropped it. England amateur international Ken Gray scored the only goal of the game. Ten minutes later, Chesham missed their last chance: Kenny Kent's penalty. It was their only appearance in the final.

No-one could write a section like this without an honourable mention for Gary Sprake, whose generosity was legendary. They played *Careless Hands* over the tannoy after he'd thrown the ball into his own net at Anfield. They cheered him to the rafters when he let the ball slip out of his grasp for Chivers to score the only goal of the game at White Hart Lane. He won 37 Welsh caps spread over exactly 11 years and spent a decade as first choice of the best club in the country, so it wasn't all head in hands. But . . .

By 1970, Leeds had never won the FA Cup. In the final, they took a lucky lead over Chelsea and ran the match, Eddie Gray doing embarrassing things to David Webb. Then, four minutes from half-time, McCreadie's lob was glanced on by Hutchison to Peter Houseman wide on the left. Houseman shot with no power to Sprake's left. The 'keeper only had to lie down to gather the ball in. The lying down was fine, the gathering-in a problem. The ball went through his arms in slow motion and sat in the side netting.

Sprake was dropped for the replay, which Chelsea won after being a goal down. Leeds reached the final again two years later, winning it at last, then losing to Sunderland the following year – but by then Sprake had been replaced by David Harvey, who was safer but nothing like as much fun.

After all his years with West Ham, it was ironic that they should be the opponents when Bobby Moore came back to Wembley with Fulham for the 1975 FA Cup final.

West Ham were the favourites, but Mooro and Mullery bossed the first half. If the Second Division team had had a quality out-and-out striker (they'd scored only nine goals in their last eight matches in the competition), or if John Mitchell had scored after doing the difficult part just after half-time: if, if.

On the hour, John Cutbush lost the ball to Patsy Holland, who cut inside and passed to Billy Jennings (West Ham's own blunt instrument up front), who shot straight at Peter Mellor. The big blond 'keeper had done well throughout the cup run but looked nervous before the final. Now he dived but couldn't hold, and Alan Taylor slapped the rebound back between his legs.

Four minutes later, Holland again put in the pass, this time Graham Paddon the shot, Mellor made another hash, Taylor fed on it again: 2-0. It was Fulham's only appearance in the final.

Before the match, Mellor had watched Bob Wilson on the box talking about goalkeepers losing cup finals. Don't look, someone had said – but big Peter wasn't worried. 'It couldn't happen to me.'

Four days after winning the 1982 League Cup final, Liverpool were in Sofia to defend the European Cup. Confidence was presumably high (they'd come from behind in the final against Tottenham) but things hung on a bit of a thread: only a 1-0 lead from the first leg, a goalkeeper in his first season at the club.

Both held out till 13 minutes from the end, then the narrow lead disappeared when the new keeper came out for a high cross, fluffed it, and presented Stoicho Mladenov with the first goal. Brucie had arrived. Mark Lawrenson was sent off, Liverpool lost in extra time.

Right: *If the cap more or less fits . . . wear it for a bet, or as a penance for losing two European Cups* (Colorsport)

Next season: an encore. Another European Cup quarter-final, again away from home (Widzew Lodz), another high cross, another Grobbelaar misjudgment. Trying to take it one-handed, he dropped it and Miroslaw Tlokinski tapped it in. Again Liverpool lost 2-0.

Go easy on the jungle man: he was only following in a tradition. For the past 30 years, Liverpool's first-choice keepers have been spectacular but not always safe. It started with two big Scottish Tommies, Younger and Lawrence, whose successor took it a stage or so further.

England were level at Hampden Park in 1976 until four minutes after half-time. Then Kenny Dalglish shot from the right, none too hard, and the ball went between Ray Clemence's legs for the winner. Banners were soon doing the rounds: Spread 'em, Ray.

Six years later, by now at Tottenham, he let Antonio Olmo's very gentle long shot go through his hands for the first goal of a Cup-Winners' Cup semi-final. Spurs drew 1-1 at home, Barcelona went on to win the Cup.

Halfway through the second half, Arsenal and Sheffield Wednesday were beginning to look stale. Hardly surprising, given that this was the third cup final match they'd played against each other on the thick Wembley grass at the end of another long English season (1992–93).

After winning the League Cup, Arsenal had led 1-0 at half-time in each match of the FA Cup final – and although Wednesday kept coming back they seemed to be hanging on this time, making few chances, needing a deflection to score their goal. Still, they held out almost to the end. The first ever FA Cup final penalty shoot-out was only a minute or so away when they conceded a corner on their right.

As always, Arsenal threw in their big centre-backs, and one of them, Andy Linighan, broken nose and all, got there first but headed straight at the keeper.

Chris Woods, the England No. 1, had had something of a mixed season. He'd been at fault with Ian Wright's goal in the replay, hesitating after coming out, and now seemed to get down too low under Linighan's header, his body not behind the ball. It hit his hands and dropped behind him, crossing the line before being kicked away.

Arsenal, who'd won the 1989 League title in the last minute or so, won the FA Cup for the first time since 1979 in the same way. It was the only time the same two clubs had appeared in both domestic cup finals in the same year. Wednesday, whose football deserved better, were the only team to lose both in the same season.

PUTTING A FOOT IN IT

bad passes

Bradford Northern, very much the team of the decade, won the Challenge Cup in 1944, reached the final the following year, won again in 1947, and were warm favourites the season after that.

In the final, however, they were let down by Eric Batten, of all people, a world-class player capped four times by Great Britain. Early in the match, he had his kick charged down by Wigan winger Jack Hilton, who picked it up to score; Ted Ward's conversion made it 5-0.

With something to defend, Wigan tackled hard and clung on. Northern pulled 3 points back – but, in the very last minute, they blundered again: a drop-out from under their own posts went straight to the second row pair of Len White and Bill Blan, who ran it in to make a try for prop Frank Barton. Wigan – who'd lost in the finals of 1944 (to Bradford) and 1946 – won 8-3.

Northern were back the following year. The 1948 final was the only one they lost out of three in a row.

Although Everton eventually finished only five points ahead of Sheffield Wednesday in the First Division, they were favourites to win the 1966 FA Cup final. Wednesday had escaped relegation by only three points, and although there were four four internationals in their team, two won only one cap each (Gerry Young and Johnny Fantham), Jim McCalliog was only 19 and didn't start playing for Scotland till the following year, and goalkeeper Ron Springett had only one cap left in him.

Everton had to replace the big England centre-forward Fred Pickering with the bit-part Cornishman Mike Trebilcock, but there were still eight current or future internationals in the side, including four in a strong defence. They hadn't conceded a goal in the Cup that season.

In the final, they gave one away within four minutes, Peter Eustace's quick free-kick reaching the unmarked David Ford, whose heavy shot was driven in by McCalliog off Ray Wilson's leg. Wednesday protected the lead by spending energy, cramping Everton's link man Jimmy Gabriel, giving Trebilcock nothing. Springett twice stopped Alex Young, taking his legs in the area (no penalty) then superbly saving his shot early in the second half. After 57 minutes, a fast dribble by Fantham gave him space for a shot which came back off Gordon West's chest into Ford's path: 2-0. Incredibly, within seven minutes Everton were level, Trebilcock making his name with two fierce shots. After all their first-half running, Wednesday were already on their last legs.

Ten minutes from time, West's punt upfield went straight to Gerry Young just inside his own half. At any other time, he'd have trapped it without a thought. At Wembley, in front of 100000, he made one of the famous Cup Final errors. The ball seemed to scoot under his foot into the path of Temple, who ran on and shot uncompromisingly past Springett.

Everton were the first team since 1953 to win the FA Cup after being two down in the final. Wednesday didn't reach the final again till 1993 (when Young & Co were inevitably paraded on television) and haven't won the Cup since 1935.

The reputation of the 1971 British Lions rests almost wholly on the backs, who were among the best of all time: Edwards and John, Gibson, Duckham and Gerald Davies, JPR. They won all of their first 12 matches in New Zealand, hitting some dizzy heights against Wellington: 47-9 (worth 65-9 now), the immensely strong 20-year-old winger John Bevan scoring four tries.

In the first Test three weeks later, the Lions suddenly staged the next phase of their con trick, playing ten-man rugby for the first time on the tour and tackling everything that moved round the fringes of the scrum. The forwards, especially the back row of Dixon, Taylor and Mervyn Davies, played above themselves.

Even after Barry John missed two early kicks at goal and Gareth Edwards pulled his famous hamstring within five minutes, the Lions were in control. From a lineout near the New Zealand 25, they moved the ball wide to Bevan, who cut inside and kicked ahead. The All Blacks got the ball back to Alan Sutherland, but it caught him in two minds. One said kick the leather off it, the other whispered something about other players doing the job better than a big No. 8 forward. As Sutherland hesitated, Ian McLauchlan barged between Syd Going and Fergie McCormick and closed in. At his peak, McCormick would have made sure, one way or another, that the Lions prop didn't get through. But the evil old Fungus was having a shocker, and he let McLauchlan escape.

Meanwhile Sutherland was humming and haaing on his own line. Eventually the kicking voice won and he swung his leg back, but it was big and heavy and not made for the task. McLauchlan charged him down, followed through, and fell on the ball for the only try of the match. The Lions won 9-3 and Sutherland was dropped from the rest of the series, the only one New Zealand have ever lost to the British Isles.

Things were stacked high against West Ham in the 1976 Cup-Winners' Cup final: Anderlecht were playing virtually at home, in

95

the Heysel, and the Hammers hadn't won away even once on the European run. More importantly, in terms of quality there was no comparison between the teams. Only Brooking could be mentioned in the same breath as Van der Elst, Haan and Rensenbrink, while players like Coleman, Holland, McDowell and especially the two strikers, Jennings and Keith Robson, made West Ham what they were, a team who didn't win any of their last 16 League games and finished 18th in the First Division. After the final, Rensenbrink was very dismissive.

During it, West Ham played a tremendous first half, taking the lead after half an hour when Paddon took a short corner, exchanged passes with Coleman, Robson headed on and Holland scored from close range. Soon afterwards Jennings missed an easy chance after Holland had stepped over a low cross.

West Ham should have held out till half-time, which was only two minutes away when Frank Lampard received a pass outside the penalty area on the left, looked up to hit the long clearance, then turned and passed back to Mervyn Day.

The previous season, in the sixth round of the FA Cup run that took them to this final, West Ham were leading 1-0 at Highbury when Lampard's underhit backpass let in John Radford, who was brought down by Day without penalty.

This time no escape. Peter Ressel nipped in front of Day and pulled the ball back to his fellow Dutchman Rensenbrink, who took his time, found space, and scooped the ball high into a virtually undefended net. A minute later, Lampard twisted a knee and didn't come out for the second half.

In the end, although Robson equalised after Van der Elst had scored, Anderlecht pulled away to win 4-2, the decisive goal a penalty conceded by Holland (hero turned patsy), and West Ham disappeared from European competition till 1980–81 – but did eventually gain something from the '76 final: François Van der Elst joined them in 1982.

Denmark, in the World Cup finals for the first time, had more world class footballers than any other team in 1986: captain and sweeper Morten Olsen; Arnesen and Lerby in midfield; the strong-running Elkjaer up front with Michael Laudrup, who looked like becoming one of the greats. So much quality that Jan Molby and Jesper Olsen, both with English clubs, were used mainly as substitutes.

The Danes won all three matches in the hardest of the six groups, beating Scotland and West Germany without conceding a goal, thrashing the fancied Uruguayans 6-1.

In the second round match against Spain, for a place in the quarter-finals, Klaus Berggreen was tripped by Gallego in the area, Jesper Olsen sent Zubizarreta the wrong way from the penalty spot, and Denmark were on the march again.

Two minutes from half-time, the same Olsen dropped back and out to the right to pick up a short free kick from Lars Hogh, rolled it around to kill a little time, then knocked it back to the keeper without really looking up. It didn't get there. Butragueño, lurking with no real intent, received it on a plate, and slipped it past Hogh without breaking stride.

The blunder cut into Denmark's confidence. Ten minutes after half-time, Butragueño was left unmarked to head a second. Ten minutes after that, Butragueño was brought down by Soren Busk, and Goycoechea put away the penalty. Butragueño scored two more, one a penalty, to equal the World Cup finals record, Spain won 5-1.

The Danes walked off, the shell shock showing on Elkjaer's TV interview, Jesper Olsen limping after a foul by Michel. Denmark won the 1992 European Championship against expectations, but have never had a team like this, before or since. It was their only appearance in the World Cup finals.

Above: Jesper Olsen practises his passing against Spain
(Bob Thomas Sports Photography)

Franz Heinzer's been the leading downhill skier of the last few years: world champion in 1991, World Cup winner in 1993. At the 1994 Olympics, he pushed out from the starting gate, put one ski on the other, loosened his bindings, and came to a halt after no more than five seconds and five yards. He announced his retirement before the Games were over.

PENALTIES OF FAME

Gary Lineker began the 1991–92 football season needing to score five goals to break Bobby Charlton's England record of 49. His volley against Poland took England to the European finals, he scored against France and the CIS, and went into the game against Brazil at Wembley needing just one more to match Charlton.

After only ten minutes, chasing a ball into the right-hand side of the area, he went round the goalkeeper, 36-year-old Carlos Gallo, who may or may not have got a touch to Lineker's head. Scottish referee Jim McCluskey gave the penalty.

Lineker had scored four times from the spot for England, earning each one (either by being fouled or forcing a handball), sending the 'keeper the wrong way each time. He did the same here, but there was more to it than that.

Lineker had missed from the spot in the League that season, and his last penalty at Wembley, in the 1991 FA Cup final, had been saved by Mark Crossley. Plus, in the recent League Cup semi-final, also against Forest, he'd suddenly hit a very soft chip into the middle of the net while Crossley dived. It looked unnecessarily cute at best, positively dangerous if the keeper didn't move.

Carlos obviously hadn't had recourse to a video of the semi-final. He threw himself to the right as Lineker ran up. Again it was the chip – but this time, perhaps through nerves, he kicked the ground. Carlos, who was already on it, had time to get back up and make an easy save from what ended as a feeble little shot.

Below: *Gary Lineker makes Bobby Charlton's day* (Bob Thomas Sports Photography)

Remarkably, England didn't set up another chance for Lineker all season. He didn't score in any of his last six internationals, was unreasonably substituted in the very last, the decisive group match against Sweden, and missed Charlton's record by a single goal.

If it's any consolation to him (it isn't), one of the ways wor Bobby himself missed out on that 50th goal for England was from the damned spot.

At Hampden in 1960, after Graham Leggat had given Scotland the lead, Charlton was fouled in the area, got up, and smashed the kick past Frank Haffey, who was winning his first cap. Fifteen minutes from the end, Scotland's captain Bobby Evans handled and the Hungarian referee Jeno Sranko, who awarded 55 free kicks during the match, gave another penalty.

This time Charlton hit it straight at Haffey, who made the save – only for Sranko to order a retake because the ball hadn't been on the spot (so Scotland were penalised for Charlton's error). Surrounded by 129 000 whistles, he drove the third penalty yards wide and held his head in his hands. Scotland escaped with a draw and shared the Home Championship with England and Wales.

Charlton didn't take another penalty for England (he'd previously been successful with three out of three). As 15 were awarded during the rest of his international career, it's reasonable to suppose that he'd have made that half-century. As it was, the closest he came was by putting the ball in the net against Holland a fraction after the referee had blown for full-time.

In two consecutive seasons, complete outsiders reached the Amateur Cup final, each time losing their chance of winning the trophy by missing a penalty.

In 1967 Skelmersdale United dominated a strong Hendon team in the semi-final but needed a replay to go through. In the final, they were held to another goalless draw, this time after extra-time, by Enfield. In the very last minute, Skelmersdale were awarded a penalty, but Alan Bermingham's kick was saved by Ian Wolstenholme. Enfield won the replay 3-0.

Next year, Chesham took the lead but fell behind 2-1 against Leytonstone thanks to a blunder by Dennis Wells (see ZOO KEEPERS). With ten minutes to go, they were handed a lifeline, but Kenny Kent's penalty was saved.

Skelmersdale won the cup in 1971. Chesham never did.

Foot in mouth
"And Lineker scored the equaliser thirteen minutes before the end. Talk about a last-minute goal!"
SIMON MAYO

Needing to win their last match of the 1923–24 season, at Birmingham City, Cardiff were awarded a late penalty, which was left to their international striker Len Davies. He put it too close to England goalkeeper Dan Tremelling, Cardiff lost the League title by 0.024 of a goal (Huddersfield won the first of their three in a row) and never came so close again.

Cardiff reached the FA Cup final a year later and won it in 1927 (see ZOO KEEPERS), the same year that Len Davies scored twice against England at Wrexham, the second from the penalty spot.

After becoming the first British club to win the European Cup, Celtic had a number of frustrating seasons in the competition, losing the title in the first round the following season, in extra-time after taking the lead in the 1970 final, in a bloodstained semi in 1974.

Having beaten Inter in the 1967 final, they were eliminated by both Milanese clubs without scoring a goal. In 1969 they drew away from home but were beaten by Pierino Prati's breakaway goal at Parkhead (Milan went on to win the cup). Three years later they again drew 0-0 in the San Siro, but Inter held out in the return. For the first time, one of the European Cup finalists would be decided by a penalty shoot-out.

First up for Celtic was substitute John Deans, inevitably nicknamed Dixie, an out-and-out striker and the only player to score a hat-trick in the final of both the main Scottish cups. He was certainly out-and-out here, firing the kick over the bar. The other nine went in, Celtic were out and (like Inter) haven't reached the final since.

In September 1973, Notts County went to Portsmouth for a Second Division match they tried hard not to win. Kevin Randall missed from a penalty which had to be retaken. Don Masson hit the bar. Another retake. This time Brian Stubbs had his shot saved. Not many teams can have used three players to miss the same penalty three times. County nevertheless won 2-1.

In a 1978 World Cup with no outstanding team, Scotland had as good a chance as anyone, so much so that you could even agree with manager Ally McLeod's trumpetings, especially after the forceful win over Czechoslovakia in the qualifiers. The third match in the finals, against Holland, would decide who topped the group, said loud McLeod, but qualification itself was a formality: only Peru and Iran stood in the way.

McLeod's confidence seemed to be based on the assumption that Peruvians don't like it up 'em, that Teofilo Cubillas, the star winger from 1970, was overweight and superannuated, and the goalkeeper a madman who didn't like crosses.

In fact, Cubillas was only 29, younger than either Rioch or Masson, the Derby midfield pairing McLeod was still relying on even though they'd been in obvious decline all season. Up front,

Muñante and Oblitas were the fastest wingers in South America, faced by a rookie full-back (Stuart Kennedy) and another playing out of position (Martin Buchan). McLeod's homework really was of the 'see me' variety. As for the goalkeeper, he didn't have many crosses to deal with.

Soon after Jordan had put Scotland ahead in the 15th minute, the writing was on the wall. During half-time, with the scores level and Cubillas beginning to run things, it's said that the limit of McLeod's tactical instruction was to tell goalkeeper Allan Rough to kick the ball harder to clear the Peruvian midfield! In the second half, more of the same: Scotland hanging on, Oblitas robbing Rioch to make a headed chance for La Rosa.

Then, on the hour, against the run of play, help at hand. Swedish referee Ulf Eriksson decided that Cubillas had brought down Rioch in the area, and Don Masson stepped up for the kick.

In the final qualifying match, against Wales at Anfield, Masson's penalty, awarded for a handball by Jordan (see HANDS OF GOD), had sent Scotland to Argentina. Now, as then, he hit the ball to his left – but this time the goalkeeper didn't go the wrong way. The kick was soft and at a comfortable height, and Ramon Quiroga, who revelled in being as crazy as they said, pushed it away.

Two sweet long shots by Cubillas won the match for Peru, Scotland could only draw with Iran, and went out despite a win over the Dutch that showed what might have been. It was the last time big things were expected of them in the World Cup. Masson, substituted by Archie Gemmill 20 minutes from time, didn't win another cap.

By the time they reached the 1980 European Cup-Winners' Cup final, Arsenal were a tired team. There was probably some apprehension, too: they'd just lost to West Ham in the FA Cup final.

Against Valencia they looked the better team but didn't go forward enough even though they had the players to do it (Brady, Rix, Stapleton, Sunderland). Valencia's defence, especially the 19-year-old stopper Tendillo, kept them out.

No goals even after extra time, therefore penalties for the first time in any European club final. Mario Kempes took the very first – and capped a miserable game ('he's not as good as he looks' said Johan Cruyff) by hitting a weak shot which Pat Jennings saved. If Arsenal could put away their first two or three . . .

Brady missed the first, putting it too close to Carlos Pereira. The rest all went in, Valencia led 5-4, Graham Rix stepped up for the next.

Even his run-up looked shaky. He hit much the same kind of shot as Kempes and Brady, Pereira saved again, Valencia won their first European trophy since 1963. The three players who missed were left-footed.

In their last league match of the 1980–81 season, Sheffield United were awarded a penalty at home to Walsall. Daniel (Don) Givens, a heavy scorer for QPR and the Republic of Ireland, missed it, Don Penn scored from the spot for Walsall (Penn pen), home supporters attacked referee George Flint, United were relegated to the Fourth Division for the first time in their history.

Right: *The punishment for missing a penalty in the Cup Final: twenty sit-ups. John Aldridge feels the burn in 1988* (Popperfoto)

In 1988, penalties were missed in both the major English cup finals as well as the European Championship final and the finals of two of the European club cups.

In the League Cup, holders Arsenal trailed the underdogs Luton at half-time before recovering through Martin Hayes and Alan Smith then earning a penalty which seemed certain to put them 3-1 ahead. But Andy Dibble, who'd been at fault with Smith's cross shot, saved Nigel Winterburn's kick, Danny Wilson equalised, and Brian Stein scored his second goal. Luton won 3-2 and reached the final the following year.

In the FA Cup final, Liverpool were overwhelming favourites, the acquisition of John Barnes and Peter Beardsley turning them from an awesome side into one touched by brilliance. Tom Finney regarded their recent 5-0 win over Forest as the best team performance he'd ever seen.

Still, if any team could be guaranteed to at least make things difficult for them, it was aggressive, niggly, up-and-under Wimbledon, a non-League club only eleven years earlier, now the underdogs not many wanted to see win, a team built round the fouls of Vincent Peter Jones and elbows of Fash the Bash. Gazza, among others, hadn't escaped Vinny's clutches for long.

In the final, after Lawrie Sanchez had headed them in front, Wimbledon frustrated Liverpool at every turn, paying Beardsley their own brand of attention, closing Barnes right down. Then, against the run of things, Liverpool were awarded a penalty of doubtful provenance.

When Ian Rush went off for his unhappy year in Turin, Liverpool were expected to struggle for goals. In came John Aldridge, Rush lookalike and natural striker with Oxford (and later Tranmere). He finished the season as First Division leading scorer with 26 goals, and put away two more in the semi-final, the first from a penalty.

Now he ran up to knock in the equaliser that would probably turn the match. Wimbledon's captain Dave Beasant dived to his left with complete confidence and pushed the ball away: the first penalty miss in an FA Cup final at Wembley.

The following year, Aldridge scored the first goal of the final (his substitute, IJ Rush, scored the other two) as Liverpool won the Cup. But for his penalty miss and Michael Thomas' last- minute goal at Anfield, the club would have won two Doubles in a row.

In Stuttgart, favourites PSV Eindhoven played below form against a very defensive Benfica. Result: the second European Cup final to be decided on penalties after a goalless draw.

The first eleven kicks went in. The twelfth, by full-back Antonio Veloso, was saved by Hans van Breukelen. Benfica, who lost again in the 1990 final, haven't won the Cup since 1962.

Although Holland had lost to the USSR in their first group match, they were expected to win the European Championship final. Their class players were on form – the captain Gullit, 37-year-old Arnold Mühren wide on the left, Rijkaard and Ronald Koeman at the back, above all Marco van Basten, who'd scored the first hat-trick against England for 29 years and the last-minute winner in the semi-final. There'd also been some luck: Hoddle and Lineker hitting the woodwork with the score still 0-0, Wim Kieft scoring a freak goal eight minutes from time to squeeze out the Republic of Ireland.

The USSR had some fine players too – Demyanenko, Rats, Zavarov, Dasayev, Mikhailichenko – but the suspension of Oleg Kuznetsov left a weakness in the centre of their defence.

Holland exploited it to lead 2-0 after 53 minutes, Gullit heading in Van Basten's headed pass, the latter finishing Mühren's long cross with an unbelievable volley over Dasayev from a narrow angle, the kind of inspiration the USSR didn't have.

Nevertheless they kept trying. On the hour, van Breukelen brought down Sergei Gotsmanov when he didn't have to, and Igor Belanov ran from the edge of the semi-circle to hit the penalty.

European Footballer of the Year in 1986 on the strength of a single run and shot (admittedly a stunning goal against Belgium in the World Cup), the slight, balding Belanov had scored a hat-trick against the Belgians, including a penalty, but had been used largely as a substitute since 1987 and was in no great form now. His long run did more to upset his rhythm than terrify Van Breukelen, who made up for his hasty foul by saving with his knees. Holland, never under threat again, coasted home 2-0. Van Breukelen's penalty saves had won the European Cup and European Championship within a month.

In the UEFA Cup final, Bayer Leverkusen produced one of the great European comebacks. Trailing 3-0 from the first leg against Español, they were held goalless at half-time and seemed to have no chance.

Then the Brazilian Tita scored after 56 minutes, the East German Falko Götz made it 2-0, and the Korean Cha Bum Kun 3-0 with nine minutes left. No goals in extra time.

In the shoot-out, Ralf Falkenmayer missed Bayer's first kick, but Santiago Urkiaga and Manuel Zuñiga missed for Español, and finally, with Rüdi Vollborn waving his arms about on the line, Sebastian Losada completed the downfall (he'd scored twice in the first leg) by missing the decider. It was the first trophy Bayer had won in their 84-year existence and the only European final either club's ever reached.

A mixture of grit and luck had hauled England into the 1990 World Cup semi-final, where they were given little chance against a West German side which had looked like the ultimate modern power team, winning their first two matches 4-1 and 5-1, and completely dominating the Dutch (the 2-1 scoreline was a nonsense).

England, meanwhile, had drawn with Holland and Eire, beaten Egypt only 1-0, won in the last minute of extra-time against a Belgian team that had hit the post twice, then needed two penalties to beat Cameroon 3-2. No comparison between the two CVs.

But on the pitch: a real match. The Germans took a spectacularly lucky lead when Brehme's free kick hit Paul Parker and looped over Shilton, Lineker equalised with a cool right and sure left, Buchwald and Waddle hit the post in extra-time, and England's first three penalty takers (Lineker, Beardsley, Platt) kept their nerve.

But so did the Germans. Shilton went the right way every time, but Brehme (whose penalty he'd saved in a 1985 friendly), Matthäus and Riedle all scored. Next up for England: the fierce left foot of Stuart Pearce. The best saved till next to last, so it seemed.

He hit it typically hard but much too straight. Bodo Illgner went the wrong way but saved with his legs, Olaf Thön made it 4-3 although Shilts again guessed right, Waddle had to score to keep England in it.

The long legs shambled up, the ball went over the bar, England were out. In each of their last three matches, West Germany scored only one goal: two penalties and (in a match decided on

Foot in mouth
"Van Basten was lucky not to avoid getting sent off."
TREVOR FRANCIS

penalties) that huge deflection off Parker. Someone's *namen* were on the cup, alright.

Above: *Time to drown Welsh sorrows. Paul Bodin's about to hit the bar* (Bob Thomas Sports Photography)

Wales, needing to beat Romania in Cardiff to qualify for the 1994 World Cup finals, fell behind when Neville Southall fumbled Gheorghe Hagi's long shot, were outclassed in every department – but hit a purple patch on the hour, Dean Saunders equalising from close range, Gary Speed winning a penalty very soon afterwards.

It looked as if this wasn't to be Dan Petrescu's day. Earlier, he'd hit a post in front of an open goal. Now he was judged to have brought Speed down, and Paul Bodin stepped up to take the penalty that would probably win the match.

Bodin's left foot had scored three goals for Wales, all from the spot. He'd never missed an international penalty. He struck this one firmly past Florian Prunea's right hand – and hit the bar.

It was the start of a depressing night for the Welsh: Florin Raducioiu's winner sent Romania through; Southall, Rush and Hughes lost probably their last chance of playing in the finals; Terry Yorath wasn't retained as manager; a spectator was killed by a firework after the final whistle.

Three days later, Bodin's successful penalty earned a point in Swindon's relegation battle.

HIGH, WIDE, NOT HANDSOME

missed kicks at goal

Ireland lost their first five rugby matches against England without scoring a single point. At Lansdowne Road in 1880, they broke their duck when Loftus Cuppaidge, the big heavy Trinity College forward, went over for their first international try. He grounded the ball under the posts, too – so his full-back had the easiest of conversions in front of him.

Dolway Walkington, one of the early eccentrics, wore a monocle when he played, removing it, they say, before making a tackle. Whether he kept it on for this conversion isn't clear, but either way he 'trembled from head to toe' and made a complete mess of it.

Ireland conceded two tries in five minutes, to Sidney Ellis and Ellis Markendale, and didn't beat England till 1887.

Before the last match of the 1932 Five Nations championship, Wales hadn't lost to another British team since 1930, thanks largely to the skills and captaincy of Jack Bassett, one of the great full-backs. His team needed only a draw in that last match, at home, against a country that rarely did well in Cardiff, to retain the title. A win would give Wales the Triple Crown for the first time since 1911.

But the Irish weren't playing ball. Typically, they played the man instead, well enough to lead 12-7 in the last minute. Then the Welsh fly-half Ray Ralph broke through to score a try. A successful conversion would level the scores. No Triple Crown, but the championship as a fair consolation prize.

Bassett, confidence at its lowest after his mistakes had led to two of Ireland's four tries, missed the kick, Wales lost 12-10, shared the title with Ireland and England, and had to wait till 1950 for their next Triple Crown. Bassett wasn't capped again.

Rochdale won the rugby league Challenge Cup for the first and only time in 1922, thanks to Hull's Billy Stone, who failed to convert Bob Jones' try in the final from a good position. Hull lost 10-9, and the following year's final to Leeds.

After missing his first two attempts against the All Blacks in 1949, Jack van der Schyff lost the goalkicking job to prop Aaron 'Okey' Geffin, who did much to win South Africa the series 4-0.

Van der Schyff, a 15-stone full-back, played in all four Tests but didn't go on the 1951–52 European tour and was only recalled six seasons later, for the first Test against the 1955 British Lions.

This was one of the most vivid, seesaw matches of all time. On a baked Johannesburg pitch, a brilliant Lions back line (O'Reilly, Butterfield, Cliff Morgan) scored five tries, the Springboks four. Worth mentioning that South Africa fielded nine new caps? Sure – but the Lions played most of the second half with only seven forwards after an injury to Reg Higgins. With less than 20 minutes left, the 14 men led 23-11 after scoring three tries in ten minutes, and looked completely out of sight.

Then Tommy 'Popeye' Gentles kicked through for Sias Swart to score, and Chris Koch lumbered over for another try in the last minute. Van der Schyff converted, but the Lions still led 23-19.

Hometown referee Ralph Burmeister gave South Africa every chance, adding on three minutes of injury time, just enough for one of the two new wings, Theunis Briers, to go over in the right-hand corner: 23-22.

It was a tough conversion, out on the touchline with the match in the balance. Van der Schyff had scored his first points for South Africa, two penalties and a conversion, but two dreadful errors had let in Jim Greenwood and Tony O'Reilly for tries, and his place was in doubt even before this kick. If he put it over, instant forgiveness and hero worship.

A photographer, aiming to film the moment of impact, was a second too late – just in time to capture the ball sailing wide to the left and Van der Schyff's bowed head and slumped shoulders that told the story perfectly. Big Jack didn't win another cap, and the Lions went on to draw the series 2-2, the first they hadn't lost in South Africa since 1896.

The Denver Broncos went into the 1987 Superbowl as clear underdogs but with John Elway's arm as a real ace in the hole. In the event, he threw for a monumental 304 yards, scored a touchdown, and hit 13 of his first 20 passes. If the rest of the team had capitalised, they would have led by more than a tenuous 10-9 at half-time.

At 10-7, in the most crucial period of the match, the Broncos had the ball on the New York Giants' one-yard line but couldn't force a touchdown. Forced to settle for three points, they set Rich Karlis up for a field goal attempt from only 28 yards.

Earlier, Karlis had scored the first points of the match with a field goal from 48 yards, equalling the record distance for a Superbowl. Now, so close he tried to steer the kick instead of really hitting it, he set another record: the shortest field goal miss. Later, ironically, he kicked a goal from the very same distance – but, at 10-9, missed from 34 yards.

The Giants admitted that if he'd put those two kicks over, 'it could have been Denver sitting here as world champs.' Instead, although Elway never gave up, the Broncos lost 39-20, even more heavily in the Superbowl the following year (42-10) and in 1990 (a record 55-10), and have never won the title in four attempts.

At the very end of the 1991 Super Bowl, the New York Giants led 20-19, leaving the Buffalo Bills only enough time for a last desperate field goal attempt. Scott Norwood had kicked one to level the scores at 3-3, but that was way back when and this was only eight seconds from the end. The most dramatic kick in Superbowl history.

Adam Lingner snapped the ball, Frank Reich placed it, nobody else could look. Norwood hit it hard, got the distance, aimed to the right hoping for a left draw, didn't get it.

Instead of winning the Superbowl for the first time, the Bills were the first team to lose one by a single point and began the sequence that saw them become the first to lose three, then four, in a row. Norwood kicked 6 points the following year but wasn't there in '93 or '94.

Above: *Never mind, Scott: we'll be back next year. And the next. And the next. In gridiron's inimitable phraseology, Norwood's last kick was 'no good'*
(Popperfoto)

England, so dominant in the Five Nations championship the previous season, had advanced rather tentatively through the 1991 World Cup, losing to the All Blacks, needing a late up-and-under try by Carling to clinch victory in the Paris quarter-final. Now, in the semi, again away from home, they were hanging on at 6-6 deep into the second half when Scotland were awarded a penalty in the England 22. The kick was from the right of the posts, the wrong side for Gavin Hastings' right-footed draw, but the posts were so close it really didn't matter.

Hastings, a big all-round full-back of the highest class, good under the garryowen, adventurous in attack, was one of the most reliable kickers in world rugby (by 1994, more than 500 points in Tests, including a record 66 for the Lions), especially from long range. Now, if he scored from this shortest of distances, Scotland were virtually in the World Cup final. In a breathless silence, he pushed the ball to the right of the posts, leaving the way clear for Rob Andrew's dropped goal to put England through to the final they lost 12-6 to Australia.

In the 1988 Calcutta Cup match, Scotland had lost by the same score, at the same venue, following the same scoring pattern: 9-6 via two penalties apiece by Hastings and Jonathan Webb and an Andrew dropped goal.

In 1994, again at Murrayfield, Hastings' five missed kicks allowed England to win 15-14 in the last minute.

LITTLE BROTHER'S WATCHING YOU

Don Fox 1968

The 1968 Challenge Cup final promised to be a classic between the league champions for the past two seasons (Wakefield, who'd needed a replay to get past Huddersfield in the semi) and the up-and-coming Leeds. It turned into the most dramatic match of the television age.

It was also one of the wettest. Wembley, after rain overnight, before and during the game, was soaked to the roots, a nightmare for kickers, even when they were two of the best: Don Fox and the old England and Lions fly-half Bev Risman. They exchanged penalties in the first 13 minutes, two by Risman giving Leeds a 4-2 lead.

Two minutes later, the first try: Leeds winger John Atkinson, who made an early mistake in the final 10 years later (see LOOK, NO HANDS), covered across, missed the ball, and let in Ken Hirst for a try converted by Fox: 7-4 Trinity.

Leeds regained the lead when referee John Hebblethwaite awarded an obstruction try for a foul on Atkinson (9-7). Two minutes from time, Risman kicked the penalty (11-7) that settled the match.

But hold hard, what's this? Leeds, thinking it's all over, don't pay enough attention at the kick-off, which Hirst gets to first and kicks through the puddles towards the line. Half the Leeds team miss it as he backs on, and on, and finally over the line for his second try to bring Wakefield up to within a single point, 11-10, with the conversion to come.

The kick, right in front of the posts, is a complete formality, especially for Fox, who's at last come out from under a shadow to win lock stock 'n barrel.

Don Fox had a younger, more shining brother Neil, who first played for Trinity at 16

Below: The rain on Don's parade (Popperfoto)

109

Right: The man of the match
has little to smile about
(Hulton-Deutsch)

and went on to kick 98 goals and score 228 points for Great Britain as well as 20 points (2 tries, 7 goals) in the 1960 Challenge Cup final, a fraction of the 6220 he racked up in a career that spanned 1956–79 (excluding those he scored in New Zealand club rugby). All these are records that still stand. His three dropped goals won Wakefield the 1962 final.

In contrast, Don was given just a single GB cap (as a substitute) back in 1963, and looked by far the less talented of the two, even when he was transferred from Featherstone to Wakefield, who transformed him from a journeyman half-back into a mobile goal-kicking prop, a cornerstone of the team that won the league title in 1967 and 1968.

Both brothers scored in the 1968 championship play-off against Hull KR, but even then Neil was the more successful: a try and two goals to Don's single goal. But a groin injury kept Neil out of the cup final, which Don now had all to himself: winner of the Lance Todd Trophy as man of the match, standing under the posts to knock over the winning points.

He took a few steps back, kicked straight on, and – to the amazement of Eddie Waring and jumping jubilation of the Leeds players behind the posts – sliced the ball wide to the right. He fell on his face, finished the match in tears and never won a Challenge Cup medal. [Neil, wouldncha know it, never played on the losing side in a final]

It was the end of an era for Wakefield and the start of a new one for Leeds, who deposed them as league champions the following season. Trinity lost in the final again in 1979 and haven't won the cup since 1963, or the league title since 1968.

RUNNING OUT LOSERS

When Australia bowled England out for only 145 at the Oval in 1896, they seemed certain to win the Test and the series, especially when Joe Darling and Frank Iredale put on 75 for the first wicket.

Then Darling played the ball towards the boundary, and Iredale – with no need to push the score along – called for a fifth run (!) and was run out. Australia collapsed to 119 and 44 to lose the match by 66 runs and the series 2-1.

Don Bradman's the only batsman to have scored 300 in a Test innings twice, which would have been three times if he hadn't missed out by the smallest margin against South Africa in 1932.

In the first three Tests of the series, Bradman scored 226, 112, 2 and 167. In the fourth, he made 217 more than the next highest scorer in Australia's only innings, but his chances of passing 300 depended on how long the last man could stay with him.

Hugh Motley Thurlow, a fast bowler who'd taken 0-53 in South Africa's first innings, was a natural Number 11 who averaged only 5.33 in his first-class career – but it wasn't his fault that the Don didn't make the third hundred. Bradman sent him back too late, 'Pud' Thurlow was run out for 0, the Don was marooned on 299 not out.

Australia, almost incidentally, won the match by 10 wickets and the four-match series 4-0. The hapless Pud played in only this one Test, without taking a wicket or a catch, or scoring a run.

At the very beginning of 1959, 19-year-old Abdul Aziz played his bit-part in cricket history. Coming in at No. 8 for Karachi against Bahawalpur, he was soon called for a risky second run. Abdul Aziz wasn't convinced it was on, but as his partner was also his captain he didn't argue. Dashing up the pitch, he heard an appeal behind him, turned, and saw the umpire raising his finger.

Hanif Mohammad was run out for 499, then the highest innings in all first-class cricket, instead of a score that would have set a *real* target for Brian Lara. Hanif declared at 772-7, leaving his teenage partner on 9 not out.

Later in the same season, Abdul Aziz was hit on the chest while batting and didn't recover consciousness in hospital. The scorecard recorded him as 'absent dead'.

Foot in mouth

"Top scorer so far is Watkinson with his 50 or Atherton with his 40."
BRIAN JOHNSTON

From 50-3 in the first World Cup final (1975), the West Indies' innings was transformed by a brutal 102 off 82 balls from their captain Clive Lloyd: 291, against Lillee and Thomson at their peak, was a mountainous total.

At 81-1, Australia seemed to have reached base camp – only to fall back down a landslide of run-outs. Viv Richards, with only one stump to aim at, got rid of Greg Chappell, then did the same to Max Walker; Kallicharran ran out Ian Chappell (going for a barely possible third run) and Alan Turner. Australia slipped to 221-7 then 233-9: 59 to win with only Lillee and Thomson left.

Real irony in prospect if the fast bowling partners could win it with their batting. Mixing singles with heave-ho boundaries, Lillee made 16, Thommo 21, the partnership reached 41 – then Thomson missed a ball from Vanburn Holder which went through to wicketkeeper Deryck Murray standing back, and Lillee called for a run that wasn't there.

Murray's throw won the final by 17 runs, and Australia had to wait till 1987 to take the Cup for the first time.

Below: *Alan Turner in a hurry to get back to the pavilion during the 1975 World Cup final* (Colorsport)

The one thing Australia needed, minus their Packer players (Lillee and Thomson, Marsh, the Chappells, you name them), facing an experienced England team, was a good start to the 1978–79 series. Instead, the self-destruct button was simply irresistible.

Graeme Wood's reputation as a runner betwen the wickets was in the Compton and Boycott class. Anxious to get off the mark in the first Test, he pushed a ball to the off and ran. His partner, Gary Cosier, a makeshift opener and a big man who needed time to build up speed, was no match for Gower's underarm throw.

Australia, one down for two runs after the fourth ball of the series, crashed to 26-6 and 116 all out, lost the Test by 7 wickets and the series 5-1.

Wood, who opened in all six Tests, was run out in the fourth and fifth. In each match, one of Australia's opening partnerships was broken by a run-out.

MISSED run outs

After losing the first Test of the 1890 series in England, Australia gave themselves a chance of winning the second, an astonishingly low-scoring affair at the Oval, first by dismissing England for 100 to trail by only 8 on first innings, then reducing them to 93-8 in the second.

Although just two more runs were needed, there were only non-batsmen left: wicketkeeper Gregor McGregor, the rugby international, batting with JW (John William) Sharpe – who had only one eye! – with only left-armer Fred Martin to follow.

When McGregor and Sharpe set off on too sharp a run, Jack Barrett picked the ball up, steadied himself for an easy run-out, and missed it. England won by two wickets and retained the Ashes. Barrett, who'd carried his bat through the second innings of the first Test, didn't play for Australia again.

If Rob Bailey had hit the wicket with his throw from mid-on off the penultimate ball of the 1987 Benson & Hedges Cup final, Arnie Sidebottom would have been run out and Yorkshire would have needed a single off the last to win. Instead he missed, Gold Award winner Jim Love kept out the last delivery, the scores were level but Northants lost because they'd lost one more wicket, Yorkshire won their last trophy to date.

One of the great run-out incidents had nothing to do with Test cricket, although it did involve a Test cricketer.

Ali Bacher's recently made the news as one of the prime movers behind South Africa's return to Test cricket. In 1970, he captained the last official Springbok team before the ban, the powerful combination (Barlow, Procter, Barry Richards, the Pollocks) that thrashed Australia in all four Tests.

However, he'd surely admit that he had his finest moment during a club match for Balfour Park. When his partner Archer Wilson pushed the ball into the covers, they set off for a quick single that turned out to be anything but.

Halfway down the wicket, Wilson suddenly decided it wasn't on, called for Bacher to go back, and retreated himself. Bacher, meanwhile, pressed on, so that both batsmen were running towards Wilson's end.

Both got there. Neither was sure who should run back to the bowler's end – so they both did. The bowler, seeing them bearing down on him, broke the wicket before the ball was in his hand.

Reprieved, the batsmen had another choice to make. This time Bacher stayed where he was and Wilson made for the striker's end. When the wires between bowler and wicketkeeper became crossed, Bacher and Wilson decided to venture forth again. All kinds of confusion followed. When the smoke had cleared, neither batsman was out, both had run approximately 100 yards, both sets of stumps had been flattened, and no runs had been scored. A classic.

THOSE WHO LIVE BY THE SWORD . . .

(. . . or the boot, or the fist, or the race card . . .)

Oldham were leading 5-2 in the 1912 rugby league Challenge Cup final when Bert Avery was sent off for a foul. Dewsbury won 8-5, Oldham had to wait till 1925 to win the Cup again.

There was no score in the final two years later when Kershaw of Wakefield Trinity was sent off. Hull immediately took the lead and went on to win 6-0, Trinity didn't win the Cup again till 1946.

After only eight minutes of the 1980 derby final, Hull KR winger Steve Hubbard went over for a try – and was pointlessly fouled in the act of scoring by Hull's Paul Woods. Hubbard missed the conversion – but not the penalty awarded for the foul by referee Fred Lindop. When Roger Millward was late-tackled by Hull hooker Ronnie Wileman, Rovers were gifted another two points. They won 10-5.

Benny Leonard had been boxing's world lightweight champion for five years when he challenged Jack Britton for the welterweight title in 1922.

Britton, who'd first won a version of the championship in 1915 and had to fight Ted Kid Lewis of Britain 20 times, including 8 for the title, had been champion on and off since 1915, on since 1919, but was just short of the highest class. The smart money was on the lighter fighter.

In the 13th round, it seemed to have been well spent. A body punch put Britton down on one knee. As he complained about a low blow, referee Patsy Haley continued the count. Britton, winded, didn't look like getting up; Leonard was seconds away from becoming the first boxer to win the title at both weights.

Then, for some reason best known to himself (probably), he gave Britton a cuff on the head while he was still down, and Haley disqualified him. It was Leonard's only defeat between 1913 and his first retirement in 1925, and Britton's last successful defence.

In the last minute of the 1982 Calcutta Cup match, the first match of the Five Nations championship, England were leading 9-6 when prop Colin Smart barged into Scotland's No. 8 Iain Paxton (who didn't have the ball at the time) to concede a penalty near halfway,

Foot in mouth
"David Bryant was giving 101% in effort, which is the least you can ask."
TONY ALLCOCK

giving Andy Irvine, who'd kicked a matchwinning goal in the equivalent fixture eight years earlier, the chance to put over another last-minute long-range penalty against England at Murrayfield.

Irvine scored from two yards inside his own half, the match was drawn, and Smart went on to perform his trick with the aftershave later in the season (see DEMON DRINK). His foul on Paxton had cost England a share in the championship.

Above: Mike Teague appeals to the referee, but John Gadd's foul didn't. He walks off taking Gloucester's chances with him
(Allsport/Russell Cheyne)

Gloucester, who've traditionally based their game on a powerful pack, were expected to challenge Bath up front in the 1990 English Cup final – but when one of the forwards, John Gadd, was sent off, the rest were history. Bath won the cup for the sixth time in seven years by running up a record score for a final (48-6) then regained it in 1992. Gloucester haven't won it since 1982.

At the start of the following season, Argentina persuaded Hugo Porta out of retirement to make one last tour of Britain. One of the greatest fly-halves of all time and a monumental drop-kicker, he was now 39 and it showed, especially against England at Twickenham, where he failed to score a point in an international for the first time since 1980.

Still, there were a few plusses, some genuine potential, not least in the scrummaging power and mobility of Frederico Mendez, at 18 almost indecently young for an international prop.

Not that he was quite the finished article. Against Ireland at Lansdowne Road, Argentina led 9-7 at half-time and recovered from 17-12 down to lead 18-17 (Porta succeeding with five place kicks out of five) at the very end. Then, in the eighth minute of injury time, Mendez (who'd given the experienced Des Fitzgerald a tough time of it all afternoon) conceded the penalty which Michael Kiernan converted to pinch the match 20-18.

It was Argentina's last chance of winning an international on the tour. Before losing to Scotland 49-3, they were thumped 51-0 by England – but only after Mendez had done some thumping of his own, retaliating to a foul by throwing a classic haymaker and getting himself sent off for Paul Ackford's pains. Porta didn't play international rugby again, Mendez has a striking future ahead of him.

In 1991, the eye-catching Hector 'Macho' Camacho (flashy punches, gold shorts) started the last round of his WBO junior-welterweight title defence by throwing punches at Greg Haugen instead of touching gloves in the usual way. The gesture (or lack of one) cost him a penalty point, which turned out to be the difference between the boxers at the end. The split decision was Camacho's first defeat as a professional.

Penalty shoot-outs apart, Argentina scored only two goals in their last four matches of Italia '90, both by the electric blond-haired Claudio Caniggia, whose glancing header equalised in the semi-final against the hosts in Naples.

Argentina held on to win on penalties, as they'd done in the quarter-final – but Caniggia, who seemed to have some kind of death wish, had tried to handle the ball more than once as it went over his head. Why, nobody knows. Eight minutes from the end, he'd finally reached it, whereupon Michel Vautrot booked him for deliberate handball.

It was his second caution of the tournament and he had to miss the final. Argentina, hit by injuries and an average team even at their best, never looked like scoring without him, massed in defence, and lost to a contentious late penalty.

If the story's true, Horatio Bottomley had it all sussed. Find an out-of-the-way racecourse (Blankenberge on the Belgian coast), buy up all the six horses entered for one of the races, hire six English jockeys and give them express instructions about the order you want them to finish in, then bet on all six just to make sure.

He'd forgotten that you can never wager on the weather. When a sea mist rolled in, swamped the whole course, and forced the cancellation of the race, Bottomley lost his shirt.

In 1912, white supremacists would have been rid of Jack Johnson (the first black world heavyweight champion) but for an error of omission. The crowds who came to see him lose made for some hefty paydays, enough for him to book a berth aboard the most luxurious ocean liner of the day, only to be refused passage because of his colour. As always, it was something he could live with. The ship was the Titanic.

Sometimes – just sometimes – you try to do a bit of good instead of a bit of naughty. And look at the thanks you get.

By the time the 1954–55 Ashes series came round, Ray Lindwall was 33 and nowhere near as fast as he'd been at his peak. Left out of the fourth Test, he was brought back for the fifth, which looked like being his last against England.

Trevor Bailey, for one, thought so. With the first three days washed out by rain and the match heading for an obvious draw, he allowed himself to be bowled to give Lindwall his 100th wicket against England.

Four years later, a gleeful 37-year-old Lindwall dismissed Bailey for a duck in each innings of the fifth Test as Australia regained the Ashes 4-0. Bailey, a mere chick of 35, wasn't capped again. Lindwall was still playing Test cricket in 1960.

A ROUSING SEND-OFF

Paul Ringer 1980

Wales went to Twickenham in 1980 as holders of the championship and Triple Crown, titles sealed by a 27-3 win over England in the last match of the previous season. But things had been happening since then.

Wales had beaten France at home – but England had surprised a few by winning twice, 24-9 against Ireland, convincingly in Paris. At long, long last, the selectors had shown sense in recalling Steve Smith at scrum-half and going for experience in the pack (Cotton, Wheeler, Beaumont, Uttley, Neary) – plus some genuine insight in picking the immensely strong Phil Blakeway at tight-head prop. There was solidity (Dodge) and flair (Woodward) in the centre, the wings scored tries, the full-back kicked goals. The powers-that-be had finally got it right.

Wales had quality players of their own (Price, Holmes, Gareth Davies) but there was no comparison with the great team of just two years earlier, and only one place kick had gone over against France. England were firm favourites.

Not that form and personnel looked likely to matter very much. For two weeks and more, the press had been stirring it up: hwyl *against*

Anglo-Saxon cold blood, Welsh nationalism against English holiday homers, Beaumont to be shown up by Martin and Wheel, Cotton to sort out Price, John Scott (the England No. 8 who played for Cardiff) to show where his loyalties lay. The works.

Even very experienced players found it impossible to read this kind of thing and remain immune. In fact, several were very mune indeed. The start of the match was frightening. Fists flew at the first lineout, Hare was late tackled, the front rows were going down like bull stags. After only ten minutes, Irish referee David Burnett called Beaumont and Jeff Squire aside and gave them the hard word. Less than five minutes later, fly-half John Horton put up a kick, and Paul Ringer, an aggressive moustachioed flanker who'd scored a try against England the previous year, late tackled him.

By international standards, it wasn't the worst foul ever seen – but with the referee's

Below: Paul's departure puts Welsh hopes through the wringer (Colorsport)

Right: Hare hounds Wales. The following year, he scored 19 points for England in Cardiff (Allsport/Adrian Murrell)

warning still in the air, it was probably the most harebrained. It cost Wales a vital three points, left them to play 66 minutes with a man short, and put paid to any real chance of winning the title for the third year in a row. It cost Ringer something too. Sent off immediately, he was suspended for eight weeks and didn't play again for Wales that season. Blunder No. 1, and the biggest.

The remaining seven forwards raised their game and pushed England back. To their own goal line in fact, where the scrum wheeled, Smith was too slow to the ball (blunder No. 2) and Squire touched down. Gareth Davies missed the conversion, but the 14 men led 4-3 at half-time.

They stayed in front, remarkably, for another 28 minutes, helped by the disruption in the England back row after Uttley went off to have ten stitches sewn into his face. Eventually Hare kicked his second penalty and England led 6-4 with only three minutes to go.

When the ball came back to Smith near the left touchline on halfway, he kicked it – but again did everything too slowly. Hooker Alan Philips charged the kick down, picked up, charged on, and gave to winger Elgan Rees, *who went over in the corner. Wales led 8-6 and again a mistake by Smith had cost England a try. Blunder No. 3.*

Yes but instantly followed by 4 and 5. If Rees had been a little less pleased with himself, he might have thought to take the ball round to the posts. Instead, he put it down at once, as decisive an error as any, compounded when Gareth Davies missed the conversion again. If he'd put it over, if Fenwick or Martin had succeeded with just a single penalty attempt, Wales would have won. Instead they missed seven kicks out of seven.

In injury time, Beaumont held on to a low pass from Smith and gave it to Paul Dodge who set up a ruck on the right-hand touchline, where Holmes was penalised for going over the ball. Blunder No. You Name It. From a tight angle, on the unhelpful side of the pitch, in the last seconds, under horrible pressure, Hare kicked the goal of his life and the lucky Anglo-Saxons beat the outnumbered boys from the valleys without scoring a try.

A month later they scored five in beating Scotland 30-18 to win the Grand Slam for the first time since 1957. Wales lost to Ireland and finished four points behind England.

THE RAVING NEEDLE

Drugs have been a part of many (most?) sports for years. If they're a Bad Thing, cycling, weightlifting, athletics and the geegees are real curate's eggs. With takers generally being in advance of testers, you usually have to make mistakes to get caught . . .

The most famous of all was made by Ben Johnson and his coach just before the 1988 Olympics.

By his own admission, Johnson had been taking steroids since 1981, but they took a while to do him much good. In 1982 he was

Below: *The bottle's up there in my room. Linford and Carl know that winning's a powerful drug for big Ben* (Popperfoto)

Foot in mouth

"And I can see the wind blowing the sun towards us."
BRIAN JOHNSTON

beaten in the Commonwealth Games final by Allan Wells, in 1984 by Carl Lewis in the Olympic final.

It wasn't until 1986 that the chemicals really began to do their stuff. His 9.95 was the fastest time in the world and he beat Linford Christie by two yards in the Commonwealth final.

The following year, he rather overdid it, breaking the world record by a full tenth of a second in the world championships. Knowing it came out of a bottle was one thing (the huge chest, bad skin and yellow eyes were classic signs), proving it another.

Then a stroke of luck. Early in 1988, he pulled a hamstring, then (much closer to the Games) injured himself again. Just over a month before the Olympic final, he lost to Lewis and Calvin Smith in Zürich, then to Smith and Dennis Mitchell in Cologne. Drastic choices ahead.

Unsure whether Johnson in this form could hold off Lewis, his coach Charlie Francis gave him a stanozolol booster too close to the final. The rest we all know.

The real blunder in this case was made, arguably at least, by the IAAF, who banned Johnson for only two years, leaving him free to compete in the 1992 Olympics, where he trailed in last in his semi-final. In 1993 he was caught again and banned for life.

If athletics has its problems, cycling's right up there alongside. The finger's been pointed at Eddy Merckx's puffy face, Laurent Fignon's superhuman climbing in the 1984 Tour de France, the deaths of Knut Jensen in the 1960 Olympics and Tommy Simpson in the 1967 Tour de France (two different kinds of amphetamine were found in his luggage). During the 1976 Tour alone, six riders were caught, including a previous winner (Luis Ocaña) and a future winner (Joop Zoetemelk). It was widely whispered that Bernard Thevenet tested positive on the way to winning the 1977 Tour.

Various Tour de France competitors have testified to the use of steroids, cocaine, chloroform (!), hormone treatments, painkillers mixed with strychnine, various cardiac aids – and implicated doctors, team mates, race organisers, the whole shooting-up match. There's always been a lot of it about.

So much so that it's been seriously suggested that riders *have* to take drugs to cope with the thin air of the great Alpine and Pyrenean climbs. Jacques Anquetil, five times winner of the Tour de France, was categorical: 'Everyone in cycling dopes himself. Those who claim they don't are liars.'

Yet so many blind eyes are turned that there's really no reason to get caught unless you make a really champion cock-up; i.e. unless you're Michel Pollentier.

Riding in the 1978 Tour de France, he bounded up the murderous Alpe d'Huez to win the 16th stage, take the Yellow

Jersey, and put it over the polka dots he was already wearing as King of the Mountains. When he presented himself at the doping control after the stage, a sizeable quantity of alupin, a stimulant which acts like adrenalin, was sloshing around in his bladder.

No problem. Like so many other riders, Pollentier equipped himself with a 'pear', a rubber bulb tucked into the armpit to squeeze drug-free urine down a tube which fitted snugly between the buttocks and emerged under the penis. No bed of roses, but apparently good at its job.

Good, that is, if the rider knew how to operate the bulb. Pollentier found it damned inconvenient. This was the first time he'd ever worn the Yellow Jersey, so he hadn't had much practice. Perhaps his armpit muscles weren't strong enough. Either way, the doctor grew impatient, then suspicious, then pulled Pollentier's shorts down to expose his little pipe. He was stripped (of the Yellow Jersey too) and disqualified from the Tour, which he never won.

Willie Johnston's feistiness (he was sent off fifteen times in his senior career) was an important ingredient in making him one of the most dangerous wingers in British football for more than a decade. First capped at 18 in 1965, he was recalled in 1977 after a six-year gap, in time to become an important part of the Scotland team that qualified for the 1978 World Cup finals.

Once there, before the opening match against Peru, Johnston took one of the asthma tablets prescribed for him by Dr Roger Pinner at West Brom. He made no secret of it: the bottle was in full view in his room.

All well and good (sort of), but he'd made the mistake of not informing team officials that he was taking something. If he had, they'd have discovered that the tablets contained the banned stimulant fencamfamin.

The affair did nothing for Scotland's morale after the defeat by Peru, they didn't reach the second round, and World Cup Willie was banned for life by the Scottish FA.

The Rick DeMont panto was similar, but with officials playing the wise monkeys.

Before the 1972 Olympics, swimmer DeMont was only 16 but already the world record holder at 1500m freestyle. In the 400m, three days before his main event, he was only sixth at halfway but came through to beat Brad Cooper of Australia into second place by a hundredth of a second. Two days later, he qualified easily for the 1500 final.

On the morning of the race, however, he was told he'd failed the drugs test after the 400, the gold medal would have to be given back, and he wouldn't be able to compete in the longer event.

DeMont had been taking medication for asthma since he was four. The night before the 400m final, he'd woken up wheezing and taken a Marax tablet without realising it contained the banned drug ephedrine.

He wasn't the only one. After the disqualification, a team doctor rang DeMont's own chemist in California to ask what Marax was made of! It seems that none of the US medical staff had bothered to bring a list of banned drugs to the Olympics.

Four years later, officials went through the US swimming team with a finetooth comb and found that 16 of them were taking prohibited drugs, changed in time for the Games but too late of course for DeMont, who didn't compete at the Olympics again.

The last word on the whole malodorous subject goes to Wally Lewis, who didn't look like a rugby league player (balding, stocky, none too quick) but was one of the greatest playmakers of all time, hub and captain of the all-powerful Australian teams of the 1980s. After a match in Brisbane in 1986, he was given a clean bill of health, which showed up some drug tests for what they are: he'd replaced his urine sample with a tot of flat lager. Mind you, embarrassed testers might say it can be hard to tell the difference.

EATING DISORDERS

(so does drinking)

Felix Carvajal was one of the great cavaliers. A 5ft Cuban postman who wanted to take part in the 1904 Olympics in St Louis, he had to hitch-hike across the USA after losing all his money in a crap game, arriving at the starting line of the Marathon in his street clothes. The story goes that his trousers were hurriedly cut off at the knee by Martin Sheridan, multiple medallist in the throwing events.

And off Felix Carvajal went, trotting through the Missouri countryside in his boots, long-sleeved white shirt, beret and moustache, making light of the heat (32° C) and terrible dust by stopping to natter with passers-by and enjoying the peaches offered to him by one of the officials.

None of this would have been worth more than a line or two if Felix Carvajal hadn't finished fourth, and none the worse for wear. If he hadn't made the mistake of helping himself to some unripe apples from an orchard (and having to stop for an attack of stomach cramps) he might well have won a medal, quite possibly the gold, especially since the winner, Tom Hicks, was slowed down by a combination of strychnine and eggs in brandy.

Food was also Joseph Guillemot's bane in Antwerp. After winning the 10 000 metres gold medal, he was expected to do the same in the 5000 by again outsprinting Paavo Nurmi, whose invincibility was still four years away.

Guillemot finished his lunch in good time for the 5.30 start, only to be reminded (he'd forgotten) that the race had been brought forward to 2.15. He held out long enough to overtake Nurmi in the backstretch on the last lap, but the Finn came back to beat him into second place by ten yards.

Guillemots, brown-and-white seabirds that nest on cliffs, have been known to vomit their food in the general direction of would-be predators. Only one Guillemot has been known to regurgitate food over a predator who beat him in an Olympic final. It was the great Nurmi's least dignified exit.

The Davis Cup changed hands in 1946 for a variety of reasons. The USA were right to replace Frank Parker in the singles with Ted Schroeder (see PRIDE COMETH . . .), the Australians wrong

Whereas Felix Carvajal lost a probable medal in the Marathon by eating green apples because the officials hadn't laid on any water, Chris Gitsham lost a possible Marathon gold by taking the water provided.

At the 1912 Olympics in Stockholm, he was running neck-and-neck with fellow South African Ken McArthur when he stopped for a drink at the last refreshment table. It was only two miles from the stadium and he should have kept going. McArthur did, winning by less than a minute as Gitsham sloshed home for the silver.

Eight years later, in the Games at Antwerp, Gitsham led after 15 km but had to retire in pain after 35 when one of his shoes fell apart.

Foot in mouth

"Hodge has been unfit for two weeks. Well no, for fourteen days."
BOBBY ROBSON

to replace Colin Long in the doubles with Adrian Quist – and the Australian camp had some antediluvian ideas on diet and conditioning. It's always been a meat-eating country, but this was ridiculous.

Dinny Pails remembered having to eat three gargantuan meals a day. Steak or chops and eggs for breakfast, more of exactly the same for lunch, a blow-out in the evening. He preferred a salad at mid-day, but the trainers wouldn't let him near one. Got to keep your strength up, he was told. And plenty of rest. Jogging's right out.

Pails and John Bromwich could feel themselves growing lethargic as their waistlines expanded. Although Bromwich somehow managed to take Schroeder to five sets, Pails was easy meat for the voracious net-rushing Kramer (who probably ate his greens): he lost both his singles in straight sets.

While Kramer and Schroeder hunted at the net, Pails and Bromwich were criticised for staying back too much. It was hardly surprising. They were so full of animal fat they could hardly move. Australia lost the match 5-0, winning only two sets, the heaviest defeat by a defending country in Davis Cup history.

As soon as Steve Jones of Wales moved up in distance, he changed almost overnight from an ordinary 10000 metre man with no finishing speed into the best Marathon runner in the world. In 1984 he broke the world record. In 1985 he came within a single frustrating second of Carlos Lopes' new mark (almost a minute faster). In 1986, after a bronze medal in a Commonwealth Games 10000 metres that he treated as a training spin, he dominated the European Championship Marathon in Stuttgart.

Although he hadn't run a race at the distance since that near miss the previous year, he proved he was in great form by passing 20 km in exactly an hour with a lead of more than two minutes. The rest of the race looked processional.

It became clear, though, that Jones had stopped taking in liquid at the refreshment tables. Having made no provision for any suitable drinks to be laid out, he found nothing but carbonated mineral water waiting for him, couldn't deal with it, so stopped taking anything at all. Going at world record pace as he was, it was lunacy.

At the 30km mark, dehydration was setting in and the Italians closing fast. Ten minutes later they went straight past and Jones couldn't respond. In the stadium, Gelindo Bordin pulled away from Orlando Pizzolato to win by three seconds. Jones, brave if foolish, finished more than 11 minutes later in 20th place.

Bordin retained the title in 1990 after winning the 1988 Olympic gold. Jones never won a major championship Marathon, but his 1985 time is still a British record of the highest world class.

THE DEMON DRINK

alcoholic adventures

Bobby Peel was the second of Yorkshire's great left-arm spinners, one of the first bowlers to take 100 Test wickets (102 at only 16.81 each), a very dependable fielder in the covers – and an equally dab hand with a glass.

More than once, *Wisden* recorded him playing while well lubricated. In one match, the Yorkshire captain Martin Hawke dropped him from the team after he'd run the wrong way and bowled at the pavilion instead of the batsman. The famous last straw broke the back in 1897, a year after his 6-23 had bowled Australia out for 44.

The morning after making his highest ever first-class score, 210 not out against Warwickshire, and sharing in an eighth wicket partnership of 262 with Hawke, the story (convincingly told) goes that he relieved himself on the pitch and was banished from the field. He didn't darken Yorkshire or England doors again.

By the halfway mark in the 1908 Olympic Marathon, Charles Hefferon of South Africa had moved up to second behind Jack Price. Soon afterwards, he overtook the British runner, who dropped out altogether. After 18 miles, Hefferon had a hefty 3 min 18 sec lead over Dorando Pietri of Italy. Two miles later he'd widened the gap by another 34 seconds. Only two miles from the White City stadium, he was still well in the lead and the gold medal looked a formality.

Then, unaccountably, he reached out and took a glass of champagne offered by a spectator. Less than a mile from the stadium, surprise surprise, he was hit by dizziness and stomach cramps, had to slow down drastically, and was passed by Dorando (who was disqualified) and little Johnny Hayes of the USA, who set an inaugural world record in taking the gold. Hefferon, less than 50 seconds behind, had to settle, light-headedly, for silver.

In the years immediately after the first world war, Randolph Lycett was the best British male tennis player at a time when it meant something (he learned his tennis in Australia, but let that pass). Wimbledon doubles champion three years in a row with three different partners, he was only slightly less of a force in singles.

Foot in mouth
"I want to be able to walk the streets of London anywhere in the world."
LLOYD
HONEYGHAN

In the 1921 Wimbledon quarter-final, he led the dashing little Japanese, Zenzo Shimidzu, by two sets to one but was beginning to tire (he was very nearly 35). To boost his strength, he took to sampling the bottles of champagne and brandy he'd taken on court.

It was a hot day. In front of a polite opponent and a crowd that looked the other way, he somehow contrived two match points, but Shimidzu won 10-8 in the fifth.

The following year Lycett reached the challenge round, the match for the title itself, losing soberly and in straight sets to the 1919 champion Gerald Patterson.

Pat O'Callaghan, who won the Olympic hammer gold medal in 1928 and 1932, might well have retained it again in 1936 if the Irish federation hadn't been in dispute with the IAAF and therefore ineligible to send a team to Berlin.

In 1937, by way of consolation, O'Callaghan went to Fermoy in County Cork and threw the iron ball 59.56 metres, six feet further than Pat Ryan's world record which had survived since 1913. Again: frustration. The throw wasn't ratified as a new record because it took place in a meeting not sanctioned by the IAAF.

Nevertheless, O'Callaghan's shadow hung over the gold and silver medallists from the '36 Games, Karl Hein and Erwin Blask, who accepted a challenge to go to Cork and try to match the new mark. Just before the event, they were each offered a pint of Guinness – the same dark potion, they were told, that O'Callaghan himself had imbibed before his own great toss.

It was probably a joke, but the two Germans decided to take no chances. They drank, threw none too well, and suggested that perhaps the Guinness had been taken not by O'Callaghan but the judges who measured his attempt.

The following year, Blask (this time Guinnless) broke Ryan's record with a throw of exactly (and officially) 59 metres. The only hammer thrower to set an IAAF world record in Cork was Yuri Sedykh (86.34 m) in 1984.

The Swedish team that finished third in the 1968 modern penatathlon (899 points ahead of the fourth-placed French) lost the Olympic bronze medals when Hans-Gunnar Liljenvall was found to have too much alcohol in his system.

He wasn't by any means the only competitor to take a few nips to control his nerves before the shooting event, but an extra bottle of beer (he drank two in all) made the difference. Four years later, Sweden (and Liljenvall) finished fifth.

During the 1950 Tour de France, Abdelkader Zaag was struggling towards Nîmes when he accepted some spectatorial assistance. It was hot, Zaag was dry, the wine bottle was inviting.

Zaag drank so much he fell off, but he was made of determined stuff: getting back on the bike, he set off at great speed – in the wrong direction. A major hiccup.

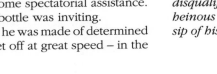

In 1991, 15-year-old Chris Almond shot 74 to reach the final of a schools golf tournament in Florida, only to be disqualified for the heinous crime of taking a sip of his father's beer.

Football manager Lawrie McMenemy was breathalysed by police near Southampton in 1980, not a great advert for the alcohol-free lager he promoted in TV commercials.

A month after his fateful last-minute foul against Scotland (see THOSE WHO LIVE BY THE SWORD . . .), Colin Smart had plenty to celebrate on 20 February 1982. A respected prop (an Englishman good enough to play his club rugby in Wales), he'd just made the final pass to set up John Carleton for England's second try in Paris and confirm a surprise 27-15 win. Now, at the post-match banquet, he set about enjoying himself to the full.

The England team was seated at two tables. In front of each player, the traditional gift provided by the French RFU, in this case a bottle of expensive aftershave.

Maurice Colclough, the giant England lock who played for Angoulême, emptied the contents of his bottle and substituted them with white wine, then stood up and challenged anyone to follow his lead in downing the tempting fluid.

On the other table, CE Smart hadn't seen the Marquis de Colclough make his switch. When he accepted the challenge, he thought Colclough's bottle still contained aftershave – and he knew his own did. Not a smart move.

Before the banquet was over, he was in hospital with an original form of alcohol poisoning, and the England selectors were formulating a letter warning the players about their future conduct. Smart recovered in time to play in the win over Wales the following month, when the one change was Nick Stringer who replaced Marcus Rose, the only teetotaller in the squad!

THE DEMON BRINK

losing after reaching match point

Willie Renshaw won the Wimbledon singles title every year from 1881 to 1886, a record six in a row that still stands (rather spuriously; he played only one match in each of the last five years) and which might well have been seven if tennis elbow hadn't kept him out in 1887. He lost in the quarters in 1888 but reached the All-Comers' Final the following year, one match away from a crack at the new champion, his own twin Ernest.

So too did Harold Barlow, one of the leading players of the day, who won the doubles three years later with Ernest Lewis.

Willie R believed in the net. To get there in good time, he became one of the first to take the ball at the top of the bounce. He relied, too, on youthful fitness. In 1889 he was 28, a year younger than Harold B but in poor health.

Barlow took immediate advantage by winning the first two sets. Somehow Renshaw took the third, but the effort drained him and he fell behind 5-2 in the fourth. Barlow reached match point six times. At 6-7 and 30-40 down, Renshaw followed his serve to the net – and dropped his racquet.

No player ever had an easier shot to make on match point. With the whole court in front of him and the Renshaw racquet lying in the middle of it, faced with an embarrassment of choices, Barlow embarrassed himself. He tried a shallow lob but hit it too softly. Willie R had time to pick up his weapon, scurry back, and swat a desperate winner. He won the set 10-8.

Even then, crushed though he must have been, Barlow led 5-0 in the fifth. Again he couldn't maintain it. Renshaw came back to 5-5, fell behind 6-5, then won the last three games to go through to the challenge round, where he beat brother Ernest to win the last of his record seven titles.

Barlow reached the All-Comers' Final again the following year, losing in five sets once more, this time to Willoughby Hamilton, who beat Willie R for the title. But for that duff lob, those other five match points, and a game or two the next year, Harold B could have been Wimbledon champion twice. As it was, he never even reached the challenge round.

In 1920, Bill Tilden came back for the challenge round a year after winning Wimbledon at his first attempt. This time, ill and tired and short of match practice, he faced the obscure, irrational little South African Brian 'Bitsy' Norton, the crowd's pet against the high-handed temperamental star. They loved it when Norton won the first two sets 6-4, 6-2.

A desperate Tilden, the brain still functioning though the slender frame was letting it down, abandoned the power game in favour of chips and chops and sliced ground strokes. He led 3-0 in the third, which Norton foolishly threw away 6-1. If he'd made Tilden work for every point, the patient wouldn't have recovered. Instead, he gave away the fourth as well, 6-0.

Pulling himself together in the fifth, he led 5-4 and forced two match points on Tilden's serve: 15-40. Big Bill saved the first, then began a dramatic rally by hitting a ground shot that just – just – clipped the line. Norton returned the ball and Tilden went for a winner, hitting far too long. He knew it, the crowd knew it, even Norton couldn't have had any doubts – but some trick of the blood made him play the ball.

He hit it out, Big Bill won the last three games to retain the title, and didn't bother coming back to Wimbledon for six years. He regained the title in 1930, while Norton reached the semi-final in 1923 (losing to eventual champion Little Bill Johnston) but otherwise didn't feature again.

Helen Wills Moody was far and away the greatest player of her generation; Helen Hull Jacobs chased her to the ends of the earth to disprove it. The press called them Big Helen and Little Helen. Jacobs wasn't that much shorter, but in terms of their relative standings in the game it was a fair description.

At Wimbledon, Wills Moody won the singles title 8 times, which would have been double figures if she'd competed every year. Jacobs won the title during one of those absences, as well as losing in the final five times, four of them to Big Helen.

In the American championships, something of a different story. Jacobs won the title four times in a row, including the 1933 final when Wills Moody (a bad loser who didn't do it very often) walked off court after going behind 3-0 in the final set.

Two years after that slightly soiled result, they both won their quarters and semis at Wimbledon without dropping a set, and met in the final for the third time.

Jacobs had lost 6-1, 6-2 in 1929 and 6-3, 6-1 in 1932, as well as to Dorothy Round in 1934. When she dropped the first three games this time, it looked like the same old story. But that win in the US final had given her confidence: she won 11 consecutive points to lead 40-0 for a 4-3 lead before Wills Moody, a competitor as well as a great technician, pulled the set round 6-3.

In the second, for some reason, she changed her game, coming to the net more often though her strength was at the back (strength being the operative word; her right wrist had to be seen to be believed). Jacobs, ironically the more natural volleyer, passed her time and again to win the set 6-3, then dominated the third from the net, going ahead 5-2 when Wills Moody missed an easy smash.

On the way to winning the 1927 Wimbledon singles title from two sets down in quarter-final, semi and final, Henri Cochet had to survive six championship points in the fifth set against Jean Borotra, who put a service return in the net on the first, double-faulted on the second, and put easy volleys wide on two of the others.

Cochet escaped to win his first Wimbledon singles title and won a second in 1929, again beating Borotra in the final.

On her own serve, Jacobs led 30-15 and 40-30 – match point – then bossed a long rally, at the end of which she pulled Wills Moody out of court. A horribly weak little lob came drifting over the centre of the net, begging to be put away into an empty court.

Later, Jacobs would write of a slight gust of wind suddenly getting up, blowing the ball away from her towards the net. Hm, maybe. Certainly she misjudged the thing completely, ended up having to play the ball far too low in front of her, and hit it into the net cord.

It cost her the tightest of matches (107 points each). She didn't win another game as Wills Moody became the last woman to take the Wimbledon singles title after being match point down and equalled Dorothea Chambers' record of 7 titles.

She broke it by beating Jacobs in the 1938 final, then retired, having won a record 50 consecutive singles at Wimbledon. She didn't defend in 1936, allowing Jacobs (in her third successive final) to win her only Wimbledon title.

With Jack Kramer now a professional and Ted Schroeder still not bothering to cross the Pond, the favourites for the 1948 Wimbledon singles title were Bob Falkenburg, a lanky serve-volleyer with a habit of conceding entire sets to save his strength, and the popular blond Australian John Bromwich, a great doubles player whose lightly-strung racquets produced deft touches from both wings (he was one of the early double-handed backhanders). Both won their semis in straight sets.

In the final, Falkenburg won a tough first set 7-5, threw the second 6-0, won the third, lost the fourth (nothing deliberate here; his big serve was letting him down) and was made to look foolish in the fifth. Bromwich led 5-2 and 40-15 on his own serve: two match points.

The first decided the match (well, one way or another, match points generally do). Falkenburg lashed the return of serve, Bromwich moved in for an easy volley, then at the last moment a little voice enticed him to let it go; it landed inside the baseline.

Still, another chance left – but there was a ghost at Bromwich's shoulder. A year earlier, he'd lost the Australian final to Dinny Pails despite leading two sets to one and having a match point at 6-5 in the fifth.

Now, on his second chance against Falkenburg, he caught a dose of whisky wrists and volleyed out. He forced a third match point, but there was something inevitable about Falkenburg's passing shot.

Bromwich served for the match again at 5-4, but his heart was no longer in it. Falkenburg won the last five games to take his only Grand Slam singles title and become the last player of either sex to win the Wimbledon singles after being match point down in the final.

Foot in mouth

"You've never been in front in any of the matches you've played, but you've always come out the winners."
ALEX MURPHY

The crowd grieved for Bromwich, who managed some consolation by winning the doubles with Frank Sedgman (beating Falkenburg and Frank Parker in the semi), and by knocking Falkenburg out in the quarter-final the following year after being two sets down, but didn't reach the singles final again.

After reaching the final in 1959 and the quarters the following year, Neale Fraser was the logical favourite for the 1960 Wimbledon title. In the quarter-final, however, he caught a real tartar in Earl 'Butch' Buchholz, who recovered from losing the first set to take the next two.

In the third, Butch had six match points. One of them was almost too easy for words (but let's try): standing virtually on the net, he went up for a simple little overhead, and did the almost impossible by putting it in the net. At 15-14 he twisted his left ankle. At 15-15 he retired with thigh cramp.

Fraser went on to win his only Wimbledon singles title by beating Rod Laver in the first final between two left-handers. He was the last player to win the title after surviving a match point. Buchholz turned professional without having made a real mark in the major championships.

It shouldn't have been altogether surprising when Jeremy Bates beat No. 7 seed Michael Chang at Wimbledon in 1992 (the little baseliner's never justified his status there) but it doesn't take much to catch the British public's imagination, and anyway it gave Bates some of the confidence he'd never had. He moved, impressively enough, into the fourth round.

There, against the left-handed Guy Forget, he hit an excellent forehand down the line to save a set point in the opening tie-break which he won, dropped service early to lose the second set 6-4, broke early to take the third 6-3, and broke again in the fourth to serve for the match at 5-3.

At 30-0, Forget was saved by a net cord which turned out to be decisive but didn't look like it when Bates prepared to serve at 40-30. On the point of delivering, he suddenly tossed the ball up, caught it, and had to gather himself and start again.

An ace would have been nice, but he served only nine in the match to Forget's 31 and he didn't serve one here. He aimed at Forget's forehand, firmly but just too long. On the second serve, he seemed to choke (he says he didn't), hitting probably his lamest shot of the match, none too hard and much too short, on an ideal length for the all-out forehand that shot unceremoniously past him cross court.

Before his weight (and Jonah Barrington) got the better of him, Abdelfatah Ahmed Aboutaleb was the best squash player still active in the early Sixties, winning the British Open three times in a row. The year before that sequence (1962), he'd reached the final for the first time, and was favourite to beat Mohibullah Khan, nephew of the great Hashim and Azam, an ungainly, noisy hitter and runner just short of the highest rank.

Even when he won the first game of the final 9-4, it seemed a temporary thing. Aboutaleb won the next two 9-5, 9-3 and raced through the fourth to lead 8-1. Then, with 7 match points in hand, the Egyptian decided to indulge himself, to make the crowd coo at the coup de grâce. Going for brilliant winners, he missed them all. Mohibullah took the game 10-8 and the decider 9-6 to win his only British Open title. Either because he'd learned the lesson, or because his opponents weren't in Mohibullah's class, Aboutaleb won the next three.

From 2-2 in the subsequent tie-break, Bates lost five points in a row, then the final set 6-3, missing the chance to become the first British player since Roger Taylor in 1973 to reach the men's quarter-finals, where Forget lost tamely to McEnroe.

Two years later, Bates suffered an attack of *déjà-vu*. Same round, court, umpire, opponent and result. This time Forget beat him in four sets.

Below: *Jeremy's chances of a quarter-final place? Forget it* (Allsport/Bob Martin)

THE TWICE MAN COMETH

double faults

They've been perpetrated from the very beginning. The first Wimbledon singles final, in 1877, matched a typical vicarage lawn baseliner of the day, William Marshall, with the long-limbed Spencer Gore, the first all-out volleyer.

Marshall had a disadvantage from the start. The net. Five feet high at the ends, it plunged to only 3'3 in the middle. When Gore took up his post, it was impossible to pass him with any pace on either side. Marshall, who didn't think to lob, dropped the first two sets 6-1, 6-2 in only 28 minutes.

In the third, adapting at last, he took a lead and seemed to have turned the tide – then, out of nowhere, he double-faulted twice. Gore jumped in, won the set and the first major singles title.

The following year, turned back by Frank Hadow's lobs, he lost the challenge round in straight sets. Marshall never reached so much as the quarter-finals again.

The reigning Wimbledon champion, Margaret Court, was back in the final in 1971.

Now, if you were going to bet on anyone to serve a double fault on match point in a Grand Slam final, it would have to be large Madge, a notorious sufferer from big match nerves. Favourite to beat 19-year-old Evonne Goolagong, she couldn't get a ball into court in the first four games of the match, losing them all, then won the next three, then lost the set 6-4.

In the second, the same story only worse. Down 1-5 and 0-40, she saved all three match points, conceded another, and this time served a double fault. It was almost a relief.

Court was the first player since 1948 to lose all three Wimbledon finals in the same year. She never reached the singles final again.

Wimbledon's centenary final (1977) was one of the best. Bjorn Borg, the holder, lost the first set to Jimmy Connors but swept through the next two 6-2, 6-1, his topspin doing terrible things to Jimbo's approach shots, and reached two break points at 4-4 in the fourth.

He missed them both. Worse, at 5-6 he double-faulted on set point, enough to break anyone's heart.

Foot in mouth
"This would have been Senna's third in a row had he won the two before."
MURRAY WALKER

In squash, if you put your serve out of court, you lose the point. No second chances. A single fault, as it were.

In 1991 Lisa Opie became the first British woman to win the British Open for 30 years – but otherwise, at the highest level, she was the game's nearly woman: defeats in the final of the world championship twice and the British Open four times (three in a row 1982–84).

In the quarter-final of the 1983 worlds, she matched reigning champion Rhonda Thorne shot for shot, serving for the match at 9-8 in the fifth and final game – only to hit her serve out. Thorne won 10-9.

In the final of the team event, Opie led Thorne 5-0 and had match ball at 8-7 in the fifth game of the deciding match – and lost the last two games 10-8, 10-8. Australia won the title.

But Borg, of course, had an ice cube where other players have blood and doubts. He played stern, flawless tennis to win the first four games of the final set, and even the Connors heart, definitely full of red blood, didn't seem to be enough this time.

Spoken too soon. He held serve in the fifth game, broke Borg twice, levelled at 4-4, won the first point of the next game, and ambled across to serve out for a 5-4 lead. Then, astoundingly ('Where did that come from?' he asked later), he served a double, only his second of the match. He didn't win another point.

JC had to wait till 1982 for his second title, eight years after his first. He became one of the game's perennials, reaching a US Open semi-final in his dotage, charming a public he'd once niggled. But (even after winning the first set 6-0 in 1981) he never beat Borg at Wimbledon.

Nobody counted the number of service winners Goran Ivanisevic sent down during his assault on Wimbledon '92, probably because nobody saw them all go by. They did catch sight of the number of aces (206) that ended many of the points on his serve before you could say unprecedented. All made with the simplest action imaginable: no bouncing of the ball, just put it there above the right eye, swing the left arm, and watch the backstops billow. In a battle of the big serves, he blew Pete Sampras away in the semi.

In the final, however, his irresistible force met the unmoveable Agassi, whose return of serve had been at a consistently higher standard than anyone in the history of the championships. No backlift to speak of, just a slap either side of the incoming server. Neither Becker nor McEnroe had been able to cope.

It was the classic final: server v returner, tall dark and brooding v short hairy and whiter than white. Tall and dark took the first set on a tie-break, short and white the next two 6-4, tall and dark the fourth 6-1 to swing things back his way.

Nevertheless, Agassi hung on through the final set, saving a break point at 3-4, going 5-4 ahead with Ivanisevic to serve. Nothing had prepared people for what happened next. After 37 aces in the final alone, a Centre Court record, Goran now hit two successive double faults to go 0-30 down.

Even then, with that .22 of a left arm, the odds on holding serve were at least 50-50. Indeed, he pulled back to 30-30. Even when Agassi reached match point, there was every chance. But the first serve went into the net, the second came straight back at him. Ivanisevic netted the backhand volley.

He's got the game (and he's young enough) to come again, but it's possible that those two double faults spoiled his best Wimbledon chance.

The Czechoslovakian conveyor belt just keeps on rolling: Navratilova, Mandlikova, Sukova, now Jana Novotna, for several years one of the very best doubles players, who broke through in singles during 1993.

Not before time, they said. The girl's always had the game for Wimbledon: mobility, good serve, waspish volleys. It's all been in the mind, you know.

Well, for once the brain took a back seat and let the instinctive talent drive her all the way to the Wimbledon final, where she recovered from losing the first set tie-break to win 10 of the next 12 games to lead 6-1, 4-1 with her serve to come.

She reached 40-30, a point for 5-1 and surely no way back for Graf. And then the brain leaned over and reminded all that talent of the score. Novotna double-faulted and dropped her serve.

That, already, was that. In the next game, she had two points for a 5-2 lead: Graf saved one with an ace but Novotna made a volleying error on the second. At 5-4 down, Novotna hit a backhand wide, a backhand long, a backhand approach into the net. Graf won the 100th Wimbledon women's singles title (her third in a row and fifth in all) with a smash.

Novotna had lost the last five games. Later, she lost in the doubles final for the third successive year after winning the two before that.

Queen of the two-timers, however, was the remarkable MH de Amorim of Brazil, who began her first match at Wimbledon in 1957 by serving 17 (seventeen) double faults in a row! She steadied her nerve to take the second set, but lost 6-3, 4-6, 6-1 to LBE Thung of Holland.

Below: *After the Wimbledon final, Jana Novotna gets all the royal sympathy she can take* (Allsport/Chris Cole)

STRIKING IT POOR

false strokes with bat, racquet and club

From 1854 to 1869, George Wells took 69 wickets for Sussex at only 17.64, which was higher than his batting average – so his feat against Kent in 1866 wasn't quite the surprise it seems.

As the bowler ran in, Wells stepped back, took aim, swung his blade – and hit his own wicket, thereby joining that exclusive band of brothers dismissed by a ball that was never actually delivered!

By 1927, Bill Tilden was 34 and coming down from the heights just as the four French 'Musketeers' were reaching their peak. Tilden never lost to Jean Borotra outdoors, and Toto Brugnon was mainly a doubles player – but Henri Cochet and the tenacious baseliner René Lacoste beat Big Bill regularly (see OH, REF): Lacoste in the Davis Cup in 1926 and 1927, the US and French finals of 1927 and at Wimbledon in 1928, Cochet in the Davis Cup in 1928–29–30 and Wimbledon in 1929.

It wasn't all one way, however. Tilden, wonderful even in decline, beat them both in the Davis Cup (Lacoste twice) and Cochet in the French – but he knew only too well that the younger generation had closed in. To beat them at all, he had to go for the quick kill.

In the 1927 Wimbledon semi-final, he did just that against Cochet, who had no answer to the Tilden ground strokes and cannonball serves. Big Bill won the first two sets and led 5-1 in the third. Playing at Wimbledon for the first time since winning the singles in 1921, it was as if he'd never been away.

Except for two things. Firstly, Cochet had a habit of coming back from ridiculous deficits: he'd been two sets down to Frank Hunter in the quarter-final. Secondly, he played a kind of tennis Tilden couldn't quite fathom, standing preposterously in mid-court, using the half-volley as if it were an easy stroke. Only when they both turned professional did Big Bill work him out.

Back in 1927, he hadn't tried to; he simply blew him away. Now, even at two sets to love and 5-1, he didn't allow himself to slacken off. With the score at 15-all on Cochet's serve, Tilden went for three outright winners, and missed them all.

Never mind. The cannonball was still to come. Even at 34, nobody served like Big Bill. Unfortunately, this time nor did he. The next time he won a point, he was 0-30 down at 5-5. Cochet had won 17 points in a row.

There was talk of the great man showing off his shots in front of the king of Spain, but even a top snob like Tilden wouldn't have sacrificed 17 points and a set for royalty. He couldn't afford to. Still blazing away to reduce the length of the rallies, he lost the last three sets 7-5, 6-4, 6-3.

Cochet, the master escapologist, won the final (see THE DEMON BRINK) to become the only player to take the singles title after being two sets down in quarter-final, semi, and final. Tilden lost in the semi-final in each of the next two years (to Cochet in 1929) but won the title in 1930, at 37 the oldest player to do so after playing through the whole tournament.

Harry Bradshaw was one of the golfing greats, a true original. A hearty Irishman often on the fringes of real success despite a weird grip and flat swing, he shot the best score in the qualifying rounds of the 1949 British Open and had every chance of winning the event itself.

Then came his stroke of genius. At the 5th hole in the second round, he hit a sand wedge into the rough, where the ball came to rest among some broken glass (a posed photograph showed it inside a beer bottle, but the facts are fun enough without that).

Now, all Harry had to do was wait for an official to arrive, take a free drop, and carry on as if nothing had happened. Naw, much too mundane. He took a great swing at the whole thing, glass flew many a mile, the ball only about 20 yards. Instead of a 4, he took 6. A fragment hit his eye but did no damage.

He finished level with Bobby Locke on 283 after both shot 68 and 70 for the last two rounds. There was never any question of Harry taking his second chance: although he never lost his bottle during the play-off, he was beaten by 12 strokes.

Locke won again the following year and four times in all. Needless to say, Bradshaw never came so close again.

In 1980, when Mike Brearley stepped down as England captain after the 3-0 defeat in Australia, he was immediately succeeded, amid suitable fanfares, by Ian Terence Botham.

The first challenge, against the West Indians at home, was met satisfactorily enough, England losing the series only 1-0. The second, against the same opposition the following year in the Caribbean, was expected to be a deal harder.

England gave a fair account of themselves in the first Test, restricting the West Indies to 365-7 at the end of the second day – which prompted IT Botham to decide that the pitch was ideal for batting and that if England lost on it 'heads will roll'.

Next day Andy Roberts hit Botham for 24 runs in one over (a Test record) as West Indies made 426-9 dec then shot England out

Foot in mouth
"That will go down in my memory banks as long as I can remember."
IAN BAKER-FINCH

for 178 (Botham lbw for 0). Following on, England reached 65-2, still 183 short of avoiding an innings defeat. Tough – very – but tailor-made for Boycott if anyone could stay with him.

Nobody did. Sir Geoffrey made 70, nobody else more than 27. After lunch, a brief shower took 15 minutes out of the game, whereupon Clive Lloyd brought on his two slowest bowlers, Viv Richards and Larry Gomes, to hurry through a few overs towards the new ball.

There was another reason. Lloyd knew that Richards loomed large in Botham's career. They'd grown up together as cricketers at Somerset, they enjoyed each other's ability and company (Botham turned down a South African rebel tour so that he could carry on looking Richards in the eye) and often tried to outdo each other in hitting cricket balls out of cricket grounds. Two high priests of the spinners-are-cattle cult.

So when Richards, ironically a slow bowler himself, came lowing up to the wicket in this second innings, it was only a matter of time. Beefy, who'd already had a thrash at Garner, cut Richards for two, a risky shot which Boycott was quick to tut about. Then, with the score 134-5, the blood really rushed to the head.

Richards tossed up another irritating little dud, which Botham turned into a grenade by trying to smash it over mid-off, where Holding held a comfortable catch. Richards jumped up and down in delight, Botham went off to make 'that's just the way I play' noises, Boycott was caught at third slip, England lost by an innings and 79. All downhill after that. The second Test in Guyana was cancelled because Robin Jackman had been to South Africa; England lost the series; worst of all, Ken Barrington died in Barbados.

In the Tests, Botham averaged 10.42 with the bat (highest score 26), 32.80 with the ball, dismissing mainly tail-enders, then came home to dominate the Ashes series, driving the cattle harder than ever – but by then the captaincy had been given back to Brearley, who never led England against the West Indies or tried to hit Viv Richards out of many cricket grounds.

The star of the 1985 US Open golf was an ex-sailor from the Chinese navy, Chen Tze-Chung, the formidable TC Chen. And no condescension intended: he played the first three rounds as well as anyone ever has.

At only the second hole, he hit a double eagle 2, quite probably the first in the history of the event, another 2 at the third, finished with a 65, then scored two 69s to lead the field by two strokes. The second should have been a 68: he missed a putt from less than two feet on the 17th, distracted by water dripping from the peak of his cap. Still, there he was, after four holes of the final round, leading Andy North by four, playing iron golf, making no mistakes.

The 5th hole was a 475-par 4 with a stream crossing the fairway 300 yards ahead. The pin was cut near a big oak whose branches fended off shots from the right.

Chen's tee shot set him up for a clear shot at the flag. All he managed was an uncontrolled 4-iron into some clinging rough among some trees. Even then, all wasn't lost: a pitch through the gap in the vegetation would save his par.

Instead, Chen went for broke. Trying to land the ball on the edge of the green to give it a chance of rolling towards the flag, he hit it too gently and it slumped into a patch of long grass.

Now he chopped at it with a wedge. It jumped straight up in front of him and hung there long enough for his club face, slowed by the grass, to come through and touch the ball again, costing him another stroke. Still not on the green, he'd already taken 5. His next chip was too firm, he two-putted and took 8. He lost the Open by a single stroke to North, who took it for the second time, only the third tournament he'd ever won. Chen was never a contender again.

Replying to Australia's 253-5 in the 1987 World Cup final, England were going along nicely at 135-2, Bill Athey anchoring things, Mike Gatting bristling his way to 41.

The England captain had already survived one chance, hitting off-spinner Tim May to the long-off boundary, where Steve

Left: *Desperate to make amends, Gatting practises bowling with the wrong hand* (Popperfoto)

141

Waugh held the catch then stepped back over the boundary. Now, when an increasingly desperate Border put himself on to bowl, Gatting moved into his infamous reverse sweep off his opposite number's very first ball.

The stroke had brought him runs in the past, but it's never easy to control and threatens a come-uppance every time (in the semi-final against India, he'd swept the ball onto his stumps). The purists had their moment here: Gatting got a top edge which hit his shoulder before being caught by wicketkeeper Greg Dyer. England, their momentum jolted, lost by just 7 runs and have never won the World Cup.

Nick Faldo's won five Majors and wants more, but how many times might he have fallen short, à la Greg Norman, but for the collapse of others?

In 1990, he won a play-off for the Masters when the very experienced, famously cool Ray Floyd hit a 7-iron into the water (Floyd had led by 4 strokes with 5 to play).

In 1989, he'd won the same event when Scott Hoch missed a tich of a putt at the same hole. Hoch hasn't won a Major.

Having won his first British Open in 1987 at Muirfield, Faldo was back there five years later going after the title he'd also won in 1990. In the last round, a bad second shot at the 15th seemed to have cost him the title – but up ahead, John Cook, after coming within inches of an eagle at the 17th, three-putted it. Faldo birdied the 16th, then rolled up close to the last hole from the edge of the green to win by a single shot from Cook, who (another one) has never won a Major.

At the 1992 world championship, Faldo led until Greg Norman came through with a typical charge in the final round. Needing just a four-foot putt at the last, he missed. He still shot a superb 63, but Faldo beat him in the play-off.

That 1987 win at Muirfield was Faldo's first in a Major, achieved by shooting every hole in the last round in par while Paul Azinger was bogeying both the last two. Azinger had to wait six years to win his first Major.

When he did, at the 1993 USPGA, it owed much to Faldo's repayment of the debt. In the third round, Faldo hit his drive at the 14th too far to the right and finished behind a pine tree. In trying to cut the ball round it, he overshot the green. A brilliant chip saved his par – but the very next hole cost him the title.

Again he landed behind a tree, this time in deep rough, which forced him to take a drop and a one-stroke penalty. He chopped his way onto the fairway but put his fourth shot into the greenside rough. A weak fifth left him with a triple-bogey 7 which dropped him from 8 under to 5 under. He finished the tournament only one stroke behind Azinger and Norman.

PLAY IT AGAIN 'N AGAIN, SAM

Sam Snead at the US Open

Samuel Jackson Snead won three Masters, three USPGAs, the first post-war British Open, and about 150 tournaments in all. In the US Open, however, it was another story. Try as he might (and he tried for 40 years), he couldn't win it – partly as a result of some memorable howlers.

In 1939, in Philadelphia, he was in charge going into the 17th hole on the last round. Here, in trying to avoid the bunkers in front of the small green, he overshot, chipped back to within five feet, then putted short for a bogey 5.

Still, if he could make another 5 on the last, he'd finish on 283, enough to stay ahead of Byron Nelson and Craig Wood. There was even a good chance of reaching the green in two for a comfortable birdie.

Going for unnecessary distance with the driver, he hooked into the rough just under 300 yards from the green. Even from here, in a bad lie, he went for the birdie (shades of Palmer two generations later). With only that 5 needed, it was a dreadful decision, matched by the execution: he topped the ball and it bounced up a slope and into a difficult fairway bunker more than 100 yards from the green. A wedge was the logical shot here, but Snead was still thinking birdie thoughts. He made the mistake of using an 8-iron, which didn't have enough loft and simply smacked the ball into the face of the bunker.

Worse, if that were possible, was to come. From an awkward stance, he chopped the ball into another bunker 40 yards short of the green, then chipped 40 feet past the hole, putted three feet past, and left even that short. He took an 8, finishing two strokes off the lead.

Eight years later, in St Louis, he showed courage and class by rolling in an 18-foot putt on the 72nd to tie with Lew Worsham.

The play-off was over 18 holes. After 17, they were level. On the final green, Worsham put his third shot well past, leaving Snead with a 20-footer to win the Open. Alright, not exactly a gimme, but a good approach here and he'd leave Worsham a difficult putt to save it.

Instead Sam hit a shocker, leaving himself with a nasty little downhill trundle. Again he hit it too lightly: the ball finished two inches away. Worsham sank his putt to win.

In 1949, at Medinah, Snead needed to shoot the last four holes in par to force a play-off with Cary Middlecoff. No problems on the 15th and 16th.

The 17th lay in wait, a par 3 of 230 yards with a bunker at the front of the green and a lake in front of that: either you reached the green from the tee or you sank without trace.

Sam did OK. The ball landed on the front of the green, rolled back down the slope, and settled a yard or so off: a simple putt or chip to set up his par.

He putted – without noticing that the ball had landed in a very small flat hollow. It bounced across the green and rolled eight feet past the hole. He missed the putt and needed a birdie 3 on the 400-yard 18th, which was asking too much. Needing to chip in to tie with Middlecoff, he finished three feet – and yet again one stroke – short.

He finished second in the US Open four times (1937–47–49–53), third once, and fifth twice.

Above: Swinging Sam never lost his winning smile (Allsport/Gary Newkirk)

THE BLACK HOLE

missed pots and putts

Once upon a time, you had to be fit to be world professional snooker champion. Or at least manage to stay on your feet for a while. None of these best-of-35 sprints; in 1946 Joe Davis had to win 78 frames to take his last title, his brother Fred 84 in 1948, 80 a year later, 58 in 1951. John Pulman beat Rex Williams 40-33 in 1964.

Even in the late Sixties and mid Seventies, some finals were won by the first to reach 37. Twice that nuggety slugger Eddie Charlton won more than 30 and lost (1968 and 1973) and he was back in 1975 to face Ray Reardon, who'd beaten him in 1973. This time, though, the final was on slow Eddie's home turf, at the Nunawadaing basketball stadium in Australia. It turned into the closest and most dramatic of all the marathons.

It was played over the best of 61. After Reardon had led 16-8, Charlton won the next nine to lead 17-16. Reardon was back in front at 22-20, Charlton at 28-23, which seemed to be that. Reardon potted a brave pink to pull back a frame, but was still 29-25 down.

In the next frame, needing just two more for the title, Charlton settled down for an attempt at the brown. If he potted it, Reardon would need to win the last six frames. He missed it – then lost the next by going in off the black. Reardon won seven in a row to lead 30-29. Charlton stopped the avalanche on the very edge, levelling at 30-all, held the upper hand in the decider – then lost his grip. Reardon made a break of 62 to win the third of his four consecutive titles.

Charlton never appeared in another final. He also reached six other semi-finals, and even the final of the 1984 world professional billiards championships, losing to Mark Wildman by only 33 points. No Australian has won the world professional snooker title.

The most famous putt in any British Open, at least on screen, was missed in 1970 by the highly talented but even higher living Doug Sanders, whose reputation for burning the candle in the middle (the ends were for teetotallers and other assorted wimps) got in the way of some exceptional stroke-making.

Needing a 4 at the last to win at St Andrews, he hit a safe drive, then bottled out a bit. Instead of the pitch-and-run he'd been using to good effect throughout the tournament, he went back to his natural American lofted pitch. Still, a fine third shot left him less than three feet from the hole.

Foot in mouth
"You've got to have self-confidence in yourself."
STEPHEN HENDRY

Few who watched that last putt, from right behind him on TV or around the green, believed it was going in, especially after Sanders, clearly nervous, tried to calm his nerves by bending down to remove a fluff of grass.

Jack Nicklaus, who stood to finish second yet again, said it was all over but probably didn't think so. Tony Jacklin certainly didn't: he told the Bear he'd happily give him £10 000 to be in his shoes.

Sanders, body language all wrong, squirted the putt to the right of the hole and lost the play-off by a single stroke. It was his last chance (he was nearly 37) of winning a Major.

Alex Higgins was world snooker champion in 1972 and again ten years later. How many times he would have won the title but for a few missed pots (and that devil-take-it streak) is anybody's guess.

In his second final (1976), he fell behind 15-11 to Reardon, who'd won all three titles since Higgins in 1972. On the last day, the Hurricane blew through the first two frames to close to 15-13 – then, unbelievably if it had been anyone else – he tried to play left-handed during the next frame! He lost it, the two after that (both from winning positions) and eventually the match 27-16.

Next year he had a chance on the last black of the last frame but lost to Doug Mountjoy.

The year after that, against Patsy Fagan in the first round, he led by two with three to play, then put together a sparkling 66 and needed only a simple green to go through. He missed it, Fagan tied, potted the re-spotted black to take the frame, won the next on another black ball finish, then took advantage of another slip to win the decider by clearing the colours.

In 1979, for the fourth year in a row, Higgins did it again, this time against Terry Griffiths in the second round. In the fourth frame, he'd scored 45 and seemed to be on his way to becoming the first player ever to score a century in three successive world championship frames – when he missed an easy pot. Griffiths made 63 to win on the black, recovered from 6-2 down to 8-8 and 9-9, then won the decider with a break of 107 and went on to win the title at his first attempt.

When Higgins finally regained it, he owed something to Reardon's return of the 1976 compliment. Dracula, the unquestioned boss of the Seventies (six championships in nine years), made a mark on the next decade by reaching the 1982 final. Here he held Higgins to 14-12 and dominated the next frame – but age was interfering with his enthusiasm for the jugular. He astonished everyone by missing an easy yellow with the colours ideally placed, dropping the frame which made all the difference: he came back to 15-15 but lost the last three. Back in the coffin after that: it was his last world final.

Terry Griffiths' hold on the title lasted less than one match. In the first round of the 1980 championship, he pulled back from 7-0 and 10-3 down to hold Steve Davis to 10-10. Then, in the 21st frame, he pondered the last red, decided to take it on despite seeing that the blue obscured the pocket, missed, and lost the last three frames.

Six years later, Griffiths led the complete outsider Joe Johnson 12-9 with only four frames to go, then missed a simple green by trying to screw back for the next red. Johnson made a century break, another to level at 12-12, won the last frame easily, and went on to beat Steve Davis in the final.

When Fred Davis stepped out of the shadow of big brother Joe, he won the world professional snooker title 8 times (1948–56). Twenty-two years after the last, he reached the semi-final at the age of 64 and rattled the bones of Perrie Mans, a fine potter but unsophisticated safety player.

At 16-12 down, Fred won the next two frames and was within one shot of three in a row: an absolutely dead straight, wide open, unmissable pink. No need to think beyond it and use any risky backspin or side: this was for the frame. Somehow (years later he still couldn't work it out) he put it wide. Although he closed to within one frame with two to play, Mans made a 60 break to reach the final, which he lost to Reardon.

Frank 'Fuzzy' Zoeller won the 1979 US Masters golf in a play-off against Tom Watson and Ed Sneed after the latter had dropped strokes on each of the last three holes of the final round. On the very last, needing to hole a six-footer for the title, Sneed left the ball on the very lip of the hole. He never won a Major.

In his only world professional snooker final (1981) Doug Mountjoy recovered from 6-0 down to trail Steve Davis only 9-7 – then, in a frame-winning position, went in off the green to let a shaky Davis off the hook. It was the crucial frame of the match: Davis fluked the blue to lead 10-7, then 10-8 and 14-12 (which would have been 13-13 but for that in-off) before winning his first world title 18-12.

The standard Davis tactic in world finals was to take a big early

lead then hang on. That's if it was a tactic at all. More probably, his reputation won half the battle before it started.

Above: *Steve Davis, green and blue during the 1985 world final* (Colorsport)

Whatever, there were times when hanging on isn't precisely what you'd call it: he humiliated Cliff Thorburn 18-6 in 1983, John Parrott a record 18-3 to win his last title in 1989. But sometimes he was grateful for that early cushion: his 7-0 lead against Griffiths and 6-0 against Mountjoy were followed by a 12-4 lead against Jimmy White in the 1984 final, which he won only 18-16. The feeling must have been around that one day he'd be caught at the line.

White nearly did the catching himself. He pulled back to 16-17 then put together a break of 40 which ended when he left the cue ball too close to the pink. He had to play away and Davis sank a long red for frame and match. It was White's first final. He's appeared in another five in a row, but still hasn't won the title.

A year after the White match, Davis was back in the final looking for his third world championship in a row – and this time he took the tactic to extremes, blitzing Dennis Taylor 8-0.

The Irish entertainer was having the season of his life, winning the Rothmans Grand Prix and generally looking a contender for the first time since reaching the world final in 1979. Here he needed all his grit – he was 9-2 down as well as that 8-0 – and dug it out, winning the last five frames of the evening to trail 9-7.

Next day he levelled at 11-11, only for Davis to win two black-ball frames in succession (no lack of bottle here). Again Taylor squared it (15-15), again Davis won two in a row. He led 17-15 with three to play.

Taylor won the first two (17-17 now) then needed the last four colours for the title. He took the first three, then held his own in the safety exchanges on the last black of the tournament.

Not for too long. At the death, he left Davis with a cut into the top right-hand pocket. Although the angle was oblique, the distance was no problem, and Davis had made this kind of shot any number of times. Not just in practice, where anyone can do it, but in all the crucibles. Even in front of the largest British TV audience for any sporting event (18.5 million), the largest ever for BBC 2 and for any programme on any channel after midnight, you'd have bet your shirt on Davis.

The rest we all know. You'd have watched him over-cut it to leave Taylor an even easier mid-table shot for the whole caboodle. You'd have probably handed over the shirt gladly like everyone else (Davis never had the kind of applause Taylor received when he sank the black) and enjoyed the novelty, knowing that in the great scheme of the Eighties it was just a fun blip. Taylor didn't reach the final again as Davis went on with the business of dominating the decade: losing in the final the next year to Joe Johnson but winning the three after that (revenge over Johnson in 1987) – a Reardonesque six titles in nine years – without needing to win too many frames on the black.

In contrast with all this global domination, Bill Werbeniuk reached the final of a ranking tournament only once: the 1983 Lada Classic.

One of the most recognisable figures in snooker, the Canadian sometimes weighed as much as 20 stone, the result of an original approach to curing a hereditary nervous disorder. Without treatment, his cue arm often shook so much that he couldn't hold a cup of tea without spilling it. Not that tea entered into it very often. Worried about possible side effects, Werbeniuk didn't take drugs: his only medication was a pint of lager with every frame, sometimes totalling 40 a day (the old Drink Canada Dry joke). He even managed to persuade the Inland Revenue to make it tax deductible for a while.

In the 1983 Lada, he beat Higgins, Mountjoy and Kirk Stevens to reach the final, where he held Steve Davis to 5-5 before the alcohol started working (or stopped): he missed an important and none too difficult ball, and another in the 12th frame, to let Davis run out 9-5. Enough to drive a man to drink tea.

Foot in mouth

"It was a game of three halves."
STEVE DAVIS

All golfers miss a lot of putts, at one stage in his career no-one more often than Bernhard Langer. Somewhere between his win in the 1985 Masters and the early Nineties, his putting went completely to pot. When it came back, thanks to a change in grip,

Left: *A German loses the Golf War. Langer at the last, 1991*
(Allsport/David Cannon)

there was nobody the European team would rather have had standing over a putt to decide the 1991 Ryder Cup.

Europe had kept it since 1985, but were held to a draw in 1989. Now, on Kiawah Island in South Carolina, things were equally tight. The USA led by a point after the first day (the dream team of Faldo and Woosnam lost both its matches), Europe levelled at 8-8 after the second. With the Spaniards maintaining their form (Ballesteros and Olazabal lost only one match out of 10 between them), the whole thing came down to the final hole of the final singles, between Langer and Hale Irwin, the German needing to sink a four-foot putt to halve the match again and retain the cup.

Langer saw two spike marks in the line of his putt. He went back to his caddie and they decided to aim centre-left, just past the marks. He settled over the ball, hit it firmly (no Return of the Dreaded Yips here) – and touched the right-hand lip of the hole on the way past.

Irwin escaped with a half and the Americans won 14½-13½, which gave Paul Azinger the chance to make some crass comparisons with the Gulf War and Ballesteros to say that there was too much pressure out there (Irwin called it the sphincter factor). No-one, averred Seve, could have made that putt. Not Nicklaus, not anyone.

It wasn't true, of course. On another day, anyone could have, Langer included. Pressure for sure, but a bottom line of only four feet from the hole. Still, the scars healed very quickly: he won the German Masters a week later and the real thing, at Augusta, in 1993.

SPORTING BLOOMERS

and other items of clothing

When the England rugby captain Fred Stokes saw the state of the West of Scotland pitch before the 1873 international, he arranged to have metal bars fitted to the soles of the team's boots.

The cobbler did his work, but not all of it (he had every excuse: there were 20 players in a team at the time) and two of the England backs, Harold Freeman and Cecil William Boyle, had to play in street shoes. They slipped and slid in the mud as Scotland, the underdogs, held out for a scoreless draw. Freeman was back for one more international the following season, but Boyle won only this single cap.

Jack Blackham was the best of the early Australian wicketkeepers. His international career, starting in the very first Test match (1877), spanned almost 18 years. In the first Test ever played at Lord's, the second of the 1884 series, he was run out in the first innings and retired hurt in the second after deciding to bat without gloves. A ball from George Ulyett smashed his hand, he made a duck in each innings, Ulyett took 7-36, England won the match by an innings and the series 1-0.

During the 1921 Scottish Cup final, international midfielder Jimmy Bowie, playing at left-back, had to leave the pitch to replace his torn shorts – leaving Rangers with ten men and Partick Thistle outside-right John Blair unmarked. Blair's shot from outside the area went in off a post for the only goal of the game.

Foot in mouth
"There's Alan Munro. He's easy to spot because he's difficult to spot, if you pardon the pun."
JOHN FRANCOME

When the world's greatest player, Helen Wills Moody, decided not to defend at Wimbledon in 1936, Britain's Dorothy Round was made No. 1 seed and favourite for the singles title she'd won in 1934. In the quarter-final, she met Hilde Krahwinkel Sperling, a spidery German baseliner who'd reached the final in 1931.

Round hadn't tested her clothing before the match. *Tested her clothing?* Well, it matters. During the first set, Round's bra strap snapped. She asked to go off court and mend it, but the umpire didn't have the right to say yea or nay. He asked Frau Sperling, who turned the request down.

The rule was later changed to let umpires give permission for this kind of repair to be carried out – but it was no use to Round, who was made to go for glory or bust, lost in straight sets, and had to watch Sperling go on to the final for the second time.

To look his best in front of the big crowds, Manuel Dias of Portugal decided to run the 1936 Olympic Marathon in new shoes. Ouch. In second place after 17 km, he couldn't take the pain any more and threw the shoes away a mile or so later, had a ten-minute breather, then borrowed a pair of boots from a Nazi youth and ran on to finish 17th.

The following season, he showed what might have been by running a Marathon in 2 hrs 30 mins 38 secs, fastest time in the world that year.

Jack Kramer came to Forest Hills in 1947 needing to retain the US singles title to increase his value when he turned professional. In the semi-final, he met Jaroslav Drobny, who'd beaten him at Wimbledon the previous year, a Czech left-hander with a big serve and flair in his ground strokes.

Kramer, the reigning Wimbledon champion, lost the first set 6-3 and had just dropped serve to go 3-2 down in the second when the other semi-final, between Frank Parker and John Bromwich, ended in five sets and he and Drobny were asked to move over to the Stadium Court.

As they walked across, someone handed Kramer a pair of spiked shoes (nowhere near as sharp as track spikes, but certainly better than plimsolls on damp grass courts). Drobny, who didn't have a pair, struggled to keep his footing on the Stadium's wetter surface, lost his serve immediately, the set, and the next two 6-0, 6-1. In the final, Kramer came from two sets down to beat Parker, turned pro, and made his fortune. Drobny never won the US singles.

Billie Jean King won her sixth Wimbledon singles title in 1975, took a break from singles, and came back to win more titles (20) and play in more matches (265) than any other player.

In 1938 Tom Lavery of South Africa won the Commonwealth Games 120 yards hurdles title in the world class time of 14.0s (whimsically ruled wind-assisted). Twelve years later, after the war, he defended the title in Auckland.

In the final, he finished third, close behind Australians Peter Gardner and Ray Weinberg, but would have won if he'd checked his equipment before the race, during which 'a crucial button' on his shorts came undone.

In 1980, at the age of 36, she reached the quarter-final of the singles.

On the morning of the match, she mentioned to her old doubles partner Rosie Casals that perhaps it was time to have her glasses looked at – then forgot about them. She'd worn spectacles on court for more than twenty years and never had a pair break while she was playing.

You've guessed it. She led Martina Navratilova, who'd won the title for the past two years, 5-1 in the first set tie-break, lost it, won the second set 6-1 in 15 minutes, conceding only 7 points, had Navratilova 0-40 at 3-3 in the third but couldn't break serve, did break it to lead 6-5 and serve for the match, then lost her own serve to love with four appalling volleying errors. She saved 8 match points but not the match, going down 10-8.

Just before the last game, her glasses had broken.

All motor cyclists know it's bad luck to start a race in new leathers. Before the 1991 500cc world championship race at Hockenheim, Australian Mick Doohan (who'd won the two previous Grands Prix) tried to ward off the hex in the time-honoured way by lying on the ground in his new racing suit. Half an hour into the race, he crashed and finished third, one place behind reigning champion Wayne Rainey of the USA.

Doohan won the next Grand Prix (in older, less haunted leathers) but Rainey retained the title – just 9 points ahead of the Australian – and won his third in a row in 1992. Doohan (eternally cursed?) hasn't won it at all.

In 1991, Quincy Watts gave up his place in the individual 400m at the world championships to give his more experienced team mate Danny Everett his chance (Everett finished third). In 1992, a more confident Watts won the Olympic gold medal in 43.50, the fastest time ever by an athlete not banned for drugs. In 1993, he wasn't in that kind of form, but thoroughly expected to win a world championship medal.

In the final, which hot favourite Michael Johnson won in 43.65, Watts finished more than ten yards behind in fifth place. After the race, he was seen brandishing one of his Nike 'make-ups' on TV. Nike breakdowns, more like.

Racing spikes worn by 400m runners, fractionally heavier (4 or 5 ounces) than those sported by the Christies of the world, are supposed to be stronger at the seams – but these had split laterally as he turned the last bend. A Nike spokesman admitted sole responsibility ('We must hold our hands up') for a construction

During the 1991 World Student Games in Sheffield, Raewyn Jack of New Zealand had points deducted when her leotard rode up too high and exposed her limitations as a gymnast.

Left: *The opposition's chances hang by a thread as Ed Moses takes his shoelace in his stride* (Popperfoto)

fault that cost Watts a medal. He won a gold (and shared in a formidable world record) in the relay.

The great Ed Moses once tried hard to prove he was mortal, but didn't quite make it. Full marks for effort, though.

Before the 400 metre hurdles final at the 1983 world championships, he forgot to tie his left shoelace properly, and ran the entire race with it undone. He was so dominant (unbeaten in 122 successive finals over ten years) that he still finished ten yards ahead of the silver medallist. Nice try, Edwin, but points deducted for walking on water.

BLASTED CONTRAPTIONS

the hostility inherent in inanimate objects

The pistol used by the starter, Fred Pitman, for the 1903 Boat Race was a double-barrelled antique with a mind of its own. After Pitman had called 'Are you ready?', it stopped at half-cock. Cambridge got off to a flyer, led by almost a full length before Oxford moved, and held off a fuming crew to win by six lengths.

Jockey Anthony Mildmay, five times champion amateur after the war, was desperate to win the Grand National. In 1936 he'd partnered the 100-1 shot Davy Jones, who gave him a great run for it.

Leading as he came to the second-last, the horse jumped well but landed awkwardly and stumbled a fraction. To give him a chance to recover, Mildmay let the reins slip right down to the buckle – only to find them suddenly dangling uselessly in his hands: the prong had slipped through the hasp (eek) and Davy Jones was out of control.

Mildmay hit the horse with his whip, which was useless as well as painful: Davy Jones wandered to the left, leaving Reynoldstown to come through and win the race for the second year in a row. Because trainer Peter Cazalet hadn't checked the tack thoroughly enough (he admitted it himself), Davy Jones didn't place and Mildmay never won the Grand National.

Two years after the 1947 US semi (see SPORTING BLOOMERS), Jaroslav Drobny lost in the Wimbledon final to No. 1 seed Ted Schroeder. The year after that, in the semi-final, he came up against the favourite again: Frank Sedgman of Australia, whom he regarded as predictable and unimaginative.

Again Drobny started well. Not so much well as astonishingly, playing some of the best tennis ever seen on the Centre Court, his serve stinging the grass, his backhand holding firm. He won the first two sets 6-3, 6-3.

Then, when he was ahead in the third, a racquet string snapped. If it sounds like a bad luck story, once again he made his own. The other racquets he'd brought with him were more tightly strung and gave him less control. He dropped his serve for the first time in the match, and if Sedgman was predictable and unimaginative and nothing special off the ground, he was also fast and ruthless and had fire in his volleys. He won the last three sets.

Drobny, though, was learning. He never again went on court with racquets strung to different tensions, won the French title for the next two years, reached the Wimbledon final again in 1952 (Sedgman beat him and won the doubles and mixed, the last man to do the treble), and won there at last in 1954.

The 1962 Formula One world championship went to the wire, the South African Grand Prix at East London, where Jim Clark needed to beat Graham Hill (who led him by 3 points) to take the title neither of them had ever won. Nor had Clark's boss at Lotus, Colin Chapman, after five years in the sport.

On the 50th lap, leading the race by 30 seconds, Clark looked in his wing mirror and saw smoke coming from the exhaust pipes. He pressed on. The smoke began to billow out behind him. Still he kept going. But soon he was virtually driving ahead of a cloud, oil began to drizzle onto his rear wheels, and he had to come in to the pits. Hill swept past to win the race and take the championship by 12 points.

The oil leak was the work of a small bolt in the distributor shaft housing. The bolt came loose then fell out during the race, all because it hadn't been sealed in place by a lock washer. The world title had gone up in smoke for the lack of something that cost a few pence.

Clark (and Chapman) won the title the following year and again in 1965, Hill for the second time in 1968.

Something equally miniature cost Nigel Mansell his last chance of winning the 1991 championship.

At one stage there seemed to be no chance at all. Ayrton Senna won the first four Grands Prix of the season to lead the table with 40 points. Mansell had set the fastest lap in Brazil but finished in the points only once and trailed Senna by 34. All over bar the shouting.

But, as always, Mansell came roaring back. He would have won the fifth race, the Canadian, if the gearbox hadn't failed on the last lap. He won three races in a row, finished second in Mexico and Hungary, led in Belgium before the electrics failed, then won at Monza. Now he was 18 points behind but still charging, and his Williams was improving fast on Senna's McLaren: anything was possible.

In Portugal, Mansell yet again set the fastest lap, and was so far

Foot in mouth
"Ablett, wringing his head with disappointment."
JIMMY GREAVES

Above: *As the wheels come off his championship bid, Nigel Mansell thinks it's the pits* (Popperfoto)

out in front that he came in for a comfortable little pit stop on Lap 30.

For a second or two, everything went to plan. The nuts on his wheels were taken off, then the wheels, then the new ones fitted. Then the tiniest thing went wrong.

One of the nuts cross-threaded as it was being put back on the right-hand rear wheel and the gunman had to remove it, which involved pulling it out with his high speed 'gun'. Unfortunately, instead of making it absolutely clear what he was doing, the movement he made was the same as when the whole refitting process has been successfully completed: when he turned to pick up a new nut, one of the wheel men raised his arm, presuming that the gunman had finished his work.

The rest of the pit crew took this as the signal that everything was in order, the jackman let the jack down, the pitstop controller moved aside, Mansell drove on. As he came out of the pit, the back wheel came off.

The mechanics had no choice but to refit it in a pit lane reserved for accelerating, FISA had no alternative but to disqualify the car under Rule 133, Senna retained the title.

Mansell won the next race, the Spanish – and carried on where he and the new Williams left off by winning the first five races of the following season and taking his first world title with five to spare before moving to Indy cars. He left with good memories of Portugal – he won in 1986, 1990 and 1992, the last his 9th win of the season, a new record – but probably not of the pits there: in 1989 he'd been disqualified for reversing in the pit lane during a stop for new tyres.

GROUNDS FOR DIVORCE

When Reading FC won promotion at the end of the 1985–86 season, it was the first time they'd been as high as the Second Division since 1931. To make Elm Park fit for such heights, groundsman Gordon Neate worked hard through the summer of '86 – but the pitch was in no fit state for the first few months of the new season: he'd spread weedkiller on it by mistake.

In 1988, Gloucestershire had to abandon plans to play a Sunday League match in Swindon, not because they remembered that Swindon's in Wiltshire but because the groundsman had pulled the same Neate trick of applying weedkiller to the wicket instead of fertiliser.

Two embarrassing slips – but lacking the drastic outcome of Essex's decision to allow (if that's what they did) Southend Council to prepare the pitch at Southchurch Park for the championship match against Yorkshire in 1989.

Essex won, but the wicket was judged so substandard that the TCCB docked Essex a swingeing 25 points, more than enough to deprive them of the championship as they finished only six points behind the winners Worcestershire, despite winning more matches and scoring more batting points. Essex consoled themselves (but not really) by winning the Sunday League.

The decision to give the SCG groundstaff a day off to celebrate the New Year cost England the second Test and the 1979–80 Ashes series.

Whoever won the toss would win the match, played on a pitch left exposed to a typical Sydney summer storm. Greg Chappell, who protested about the wicket as loudly as anyone, put England in, they were all out for 123, lost the Test by 6 wickets and the series (Brearley's only one as captain against a strong team) 3-0.

GLOVE HURTS. In January 1994, a groundsman left his imprint on a cricket match in Kingston, Jamaica when he accidentally ran the roller over his glove, which he'd left lying on the wicket: the hand-shaped hollow stopped play.

WITH FRIENDS LIKE THESE . . . (1)

Two tennis tournaments, one indoors one out, were held at the 1912 Olympics in Stockholm. In the mixed doubles final outdoors, the favourites, Heinrich Schomburgk and Dora Köring of Germany, were under pressure from the Swedes who'd won the bronze medal indoors.

Then one, Sigrid Fick, hit the other, Gunnar Setterwall, in the face with an overhead smash, which put paid to any chance the underdogs might have had. They lost the set 6-4 and didn't win a game in the second.

A year later, much the same thing happened in the final of the same event at Wimbledon.

The defending champions, Ethel Larcombe and the Irish rugby international Cecil Parke, won the first set against Agnes Tuckey and Hope Crisp and were holding their own in the second when Parke hit Larcombe in the eye. She had to retire, couldn't defend her singles crown, and Crisp and Tuckey won their only Wimbledon title. The following year, Parke and Larcombe regained it.

George Gray of Australia was probably the best billiards player in the world when he entered the 1914 British (effectively the world) championship. He didn't win it, but this had more to do with a) having to play with ivory balls when he usually used crystalates, and b) a cue arm in the first throes of disintegration, the legacy of some eyebrow-raising training methods devised by his father Harry, who was also his manager.

Trying to make sure his son's cue went back absolutely horizontally every time, Gray senior took to rapping George's elbow with a walking stick whenever it came up even a fraction too high. In the end, the elbow became very painful, he couldn't control the back of the cue, and his game fell apart. At one time sure to dominate professional billiards, this paternal thoughtlessness (and the first world war) put an end to his development. The 1914 championship was his last.

Eugéne Christophe, the popular Cri-Cri, who took part in his first Tour de France in 1906 and his eighth and last in 1925 (a record span), finished second overall in 1912 and third in 1919 but never won it, his two best chances ruined by misfortune when he was leading the race.

In 1913 he broke his front fork-stem on the treacherous descent from the Col du Tourmalet. Since the rules at the time forbade any outside assistance whatsoever, he had to carry his bike all the way down the unsurfaced path to St Marie de Campan twelve kilometres away, where locals directed him to the blacksmith's forge.

Here, with race officials hovering, he had to weld his broken frame together with tools made for repairing horseshoes. Towards the end, a small boy briefly helped by working the bellows to keep the fire alight, whereupon race officials, headed by the tyrannical Henri Desgranges, founder of the Tour, penalised Christophe three minutes in addition to the time he'd already lost. The blacksmith's shop bears a plaque to this day.

Another broken frame cost him the 1919 race when he was wearing the first ever Yellow Jersey.

Fairway was *the* Classic horse of 1928. His trainer, the famous Frank Butters, thought him one of the best he'd ever handled, and the public took him to their hearts and pockets, installing him as favourite for the Derby. He'd gone so well in training that there was no doubt about his ability to stay the distance.

That year, however, crowd control arrangements at Epsom were spectacularly lax. As soon as Fairway left the paddock, he was mobbed and had to fight his way through a crowd that was very friendly but got much too close. The same thing happened when he came back from the warm-up canter – and, highly strung animal that he was, the experience distracted him so much that he made no kind of showing in the race, which was won by a 33-1 shot. The punters' own enthusiasm had cost them their money.

With the crowds keeping their distance, Fairway went on to win the Eclipse Stakes, Champion Stakes and St Leger, and five out of six races as a four-year-old.

As well as ten consecutive world individual titles, Sonia Henie won three Olympic figure skating gold medals in a row: 1928–32–36. The third was the most difficult; in fact, she mightn't have won it at all if Cecilia Colledge of Britain had had the backup she expected.

Colledge had taken part in the 1932 Games with another British 11-year-old, Megan Taylor (they finished 7th and 8th). Now, still only 15, she was just 3.6 points behind Henie with the free skating to come.

Foot in mouth
"There's no job in football I've ever wanted. This is the only job in football I've ever wanted."
KEVIN KEEGAN

She was the second skater to perform. Just as she was about to step on the ice, after giving a crowd-pleasing Nazi salute, the music started. The wrong music. The delay that followed cost Colledge any chance of the gold. Understandably flustered, she almost fell within the first minute of her programme, recovered well but not well enough, and finished second overall.

The following year, in Henie's absence and with the right accompaniment, she won the world title. Taylor won it in 1938 and 1939.

The 1946 US Open at the Canterbury club in Ohio was as slackly policed as the 1928 Derby, only the ropes held by a few marshals keeping back crowds who forced golfers and caddies to shove their way through.

At the 13th hole, the crowds were so close that when Byron Nelson's caddy Eddie Martin ducked under the rope he was almost on top of where the last shot had landed. The weight of the golf bag made him stumble, and he trod on Nelson's ball. The consequent penalty stroke cost Nelson the championship: forced into a play-off, he (and Vic Ghezzi) lost it to Lloyd Mangrum.

One of the best golfers of his day, US Open champion in 1939, winner of a record 18 professional tournaments in 1945, he didn't win another Major.

The goalkeeper who played for Australia against a touring English FA XI in 1951 probably cursed his parents' sense of humour all his life, never more so than after the second international, which Australia lost 17-0.

The goalkeeper's surname was Conquest. His parents must have thought it a real wheeze when they christened him Norman. After the match, the headlines wrote themselves.

Foot in mouth
"There's no such thing as an easier route – but it's an easier route."
BOBBY ROBSON

In 1966 Jacques Anquetil was trying to win the Tour de France for the sixth time when a spectator stepped out and threw a bucket of cold water over him, a time-honoured gesture by fans looking for five seconds of fame, often gratefully received by riders struggling in treeless heat.

This, though, was near the top of the Grand St Bernard Pass, way up in the Alpine cold – and Anquetil immediately began to shiver and gasp for breath. He pulled out of the race the following

day, never won it again, and still shares the record of five wins with Eddy Merckx and Bernard Hinault.

Above: *There's no way they can drop me now. Steve Morrow enjoys his winning goal in the League Cup final* (Popperfoto)

After Steve Morrow had scored the winning goal against Sheffield Wednesday in the 1993 League Cup final, he enjoyed the celebrations on the pitch until club captain Tony Adams picked him up, put him on his shoulders facing backwards – and dropped him.

Morrow broke his arm and had to miss the FA Cup final, which Arsenal won by the same score against the same team. Time's on his side (he was 22) but these FA Cup winners' medals can be devilishly elusive. Ask Chris Waddle.

The all-conquering German works teams filled the first five places in the 1937 British Grand Prix. The best-known, Rüdi Caracciola, might have won it in his Mercedes instead of finishing third behind Bernd Rosemeyer's Auto Union if he hadn't slowed drastically near the end. After the race, it was discovered that one of his mechanics had left an oily rag inside the supercharger! The British GP was one of the few major races Caracciola never won.

WITH FRIENDS LIKE THESE . . . (2)

own goals

In the last minute of the match against Blackpool at Highbury in 1955, full-back Dennis Evans heard a whistle, kicked the ball into his own net, and watched referee Frank Coultas award the goal. The whistle had come from the crowd. Luckily, Arsenal [Luckily Arsenal? Hm, a definite ring to that] won 4-1.

The season after winning the League title for the only time (1954–55), Chelsea finished 16th. In the next five years, their highest placing was 11th: a mid-table team who excited their fans and everyone else's, dynamic going forward, sometimes hilarious at the back.

So while Jimmy Greaves was finishing as Division I leading scorer with 32 goals in 1958–59, Chelsea scored 77 in the League, but conceded 98. The following year 76 for, 91 against. In 1960–61 they excelled themselves: again Greaves was Division I top scorer, this time with 41, Chelsea totalled 98 – but let in 100!

There were England international defenders at the club – Ken Armstrong, captain Peter Sillett, goalkeeper Reg Matthews – but they didn't let that get in the way of the entertainment on offer.

Top of the bill was a match against Everton, when Matthews let a long shot slip under his body, got up and chased the ball as it trundled towards goal, hotly pursued by Sillett, who had the same idea. Matthews got there first, decided against falling on the ball, turned, and kicked it clear – about two yards. The ball hit Sillett hard and rolled into the net while everyone collapsed, big Peter clutching his stomach, the rest of the team holding their sides.

Foot in mouth

"There is no way Ryan Giggs is another George Best. He's another Ryan Giggs."
DENIS LAW

Blackburn Rovers went into the 1960 FA Cup final with problems left, right and especially centre: captain Ronnie Clayton had tonsilitis, the whole team had lost form, finishing 11th in the First Division, and centre-forward Derek Dougan put in a transfer request on the day of the final.

Clayton's plan for the match itself involved holding out till half-time then hoping that Wolves' disappointment at losing the League title by a single point would get to them. It almost worked, even though Rovers lost full-back David Whelan with a broken leg after only two minutes (another in the list of bad cup final

injuries at the time) and Dougan pulled a muscle after five.

They held out till four minutes short of Clayton's target – then their Republic of Ireland international left-half Mick McGrath, desperate to stop the ball reaching the little England winger Norman Deeley, stuck out a foot and prodded the ball past Harry Leyland: the first own goal in an FA Cup final since 1946.

Deeley scored twice in the second half, neither club's reached the final since, Blackburn haven't won the Cup since 1928.

Above: The 1960 FA Cup final. McGrath deprives Deeley of a hat-trick
(Popperfoto)

After 18 minutes of their 1970 World Cup warm-up match in Madrid, Italy led 2-0 through goals by Pietro Anastasi and the inevitable Gigi Riva. Five minutes later, their central defender Sandro Salvadore put through his own goal. Two minutes after that, he did it again. All available evidence points to him as the only player to score two own goals in an international match. Spain escaped with the 2-2 draw and Salvadore didn't play for Italy again.

Having taken three points out of four from Wales, England arrived in Chorzow needing only a draw to make themselves clear favourites to qualify for the 1974 World Cup finals (Poland had lost in Cardiff). To no-one's surprise, Alf Ramsey left out Mick Channon and packed his midfield, a set-up that faced its first crisis after only eight minutes.

Poland were awarded a free kick wide on the left. Robert Gadocha drove it in low to the near post, Jan Banas moved in on it. The England captain went with him.

Even at 32, the Bobby Moore brain was still getting there first. It saw Banas' run and sent Mooro off ahead of it, cutting the striker out. But the legs had been slowing down in the last year or so (they'd never been really quick) and they got there half a yard late. One of them reached, touched, couldn't direct, and sent the ball spinning into the ground and up beyond Shilton's right hand just inside the near post.

Most Polish sources credit the goal to Gadocha. A few still give it to Banas, who didn't touch the ball. There's no doubt that if Moore hadn't intervened, it wouldn't have gone in. In his biography, he admits to an own goal.

Two minutes into the second half, his attempt to take the ball round Wlodek Lubanski let the Polish striker in for the second goal. Without Channon, and confronted by hatchet men like Cmikiewicz and Gorgon, England never looked like scoring. Poland qualified for the finals, where they deservedly finished third, sent there by the worst rickets of Mooro's international career.

A week later, the day he broke Bobby Charlton's European record of 106 caps, he was standing on the goal-line when Pietro Anastasi's shot went between his legs as Italy beat England for the first time. He won only one more cap after that, and England didn't qualify for the World Cup finals until 1982.

If ever a club's name seemed to be engraved on the FA Cup, it was Nottingham Forest's in 1990–91. After Tony Gale was controversially sent off in the semi-final, West Ham were overrun 4-0. When Gazza wrecked his knee in the final, Stuart Pearce scored from the free-kick; then Mark Crossley saved a penalty from Lineker, who also had a goal wrongly disallowed. After a lifetime's disappointment in the FA Cup, this looked just the ticket for Cloughie.

But there was an ironic slip 'twixt Cup and Lip. After Paul Stewart's second-half goal had forced extra-time, Des Walker went up at the far post, got there first, and headed into his own net: Clough's last chance ended by a mistake from the best defender in the country. Tottenham won the Cup for a record eighth time, Forest lost in the final for the first. They haven't won it since 1959.

WITH FRIENDS LIKE THESE . . . (3)

four-legged fiends

Not a catalogue of horses falling at fences, which often involves an exhausted animal simply confronted with an obstacle that's too high – but the heroic deeds of a few creatures who decided to play the game their way or not at all . . .

At Ballina racetrack, for example, a horse called The Doctor stopped shock-still just three steps from the finish line, and nothing the jockey did or the crowd said (a few hippocratic oaths?) could persuade him to cross it.

Similarly, at Belfast, a horse called Cashbox emptied a few by stopping so close to the line that it was impossible to be sure if he'd finished first or last!

Jules Van Hevel, one of the leading cyclists of the 1920s, winner of classics like the 1920 Tour of Flanders and 1924 Paris–Roubaix, was never world professional road race champion. He missed his best chance in 1928, when he shared the lead with another Belgian, Georges Ronsse, until he was knocked off his bike – by a cow. Ronsse retained the title in 1929.

In the Lord's Test of 1930, after Duleepsinhji had scored 173 in England's first innings of 425, the 21-year-old Donald George Bradman left his first great calling card in England: 254 out of Australia's total of 729. In the second innings, England were 147-5, still 157 short of making Australia bat again but with captain Percy Chapman in good form.

Dropped by a combination of Vic Richardson and Bill Ponsford before he'd scored, Chapman shared a partnership of 125 with Gubby Allen and reached 121 himself before opening his mouth and putting his foot in it. Well, not exactly his foot.

When an errant bluebottle flew across the pitch, it found Chapman with his mouth open, possibly in astonishment at having scored his only Test century. Into the captainly maw went the bluebottle, down the tube went England's chances of saving the game. Still choking on the poor insect, Chapman was caught at the wicket off Alan Fairfax, Australia won the Test to square the series, and went on to regain the Ashes 2-1.

Foot in mouth
"André Vandapole has four silver medals in cyclo-cross, and none of them gold."
PHIL LIGGOTT

The promising colt Goblin won seven races, including his last as a two-year-old (at Newmarket in 1977, with L Piggott on board) in which he broke the seven-furlong record. The following year, the Derby was run on the kind of firm ground he liked.

In the end, he did well to finish 10th (out of 25) behind the winner Shirley Heights: at the start of the race he'd been nearly 15 lengths behind the field.

Some said he'd caught his tail in the rear gate of his stall, but it seems that it took 15 minutes to load the French horses into the stalls, and Goblin had simply had enough. Before the start of the race, he fell asleep! If it isn't true, it ought to be.

In a three-way play-off for the 1950 US Open, George Fazio dropped back as the 1946 champion Lloyd Mangrum contested the title with golf's great hulk, Hogan. Ben led by a stroke with three to play, but he'd barely recovered from his famous car crash, his legs were aching, and all bets were still hedged.

On the 16th, Mangrum's approach shot didn't reach the green and his chip was poor, leaving him with a tough eight-footer to save par. He studied the line, settled over the putt – then saw an insect with an interesting sense of occasion crawling over the ball.

Mangrum put the head of his putter next to the ball to mark it, picked it up, puffed the intruder away, put the ball back, made a very good putt under pressure, then moved on, thinking he was still only one behind.

At the 17th tee, USPGA official Ike Grainger told him he was three behind, penalised two points for cleaning a ball while it was on the green. Mangrum, first furious then philosophical ('guess we'll all eat tomorrow'), lost the play-off and didn't win the US Open again. The creeping crawling saboteur was never found.

By 1971 the All Blacks were all too clearly in decline, especially among the threequarters, the likes of Ken Carrington, Howard Joseph, Phil Gard and Mick Duncan sinking without trace.

In the third Test, while the forwards again looked constantly threatening in the loose, the backs made their usual quota of mistakes: Laurie Mains missing place kicks, Wayne Cottrell drop kicks, the wings running crudely and without self-belief. Still, they managed to pull three points back with a try and put on ten minutes of pressure. Then the woof fell in.

Joseph took a pass, set off upfield – and tripped over a boxer dog. Yes, really. New Zealand conceded the match 13-3 and the series 2-1, the only one they've ever lost to the Lions. Joseph (and presumably the dog) didn't appear in another international.

A single short break cost Dee Dee Jonrowe her chance of winning the prestigious Beargrease Sled Dog Marathon in 1991. Somewhere along the 500-mile route through Minnesota, she stopped to give herself and her team of 16 huskies a rest.

Unfortunately for her, putting their feet up wasn't exactly what two of them had in mind. The time she took separating them from their amorous entanglement proved too much to make up.

WHO NEEDS FRIENDS . . . ?

. . . when you can undo it yourself

The night before the 1906 American Davis Cup team set off for Britain, US champion Beals C Wright indulged in some injudiciously heavy revelry, woke up feeling very morning-after, and rang for room service.

A bottle of soda water arrived, unopened – and Beals C, too hung over to wait for an opener, tried to do it himself with (of all things) a toothbrush!

The bottle broke at the neck and gashed his right hand so badly that he fainted. On the boat trip itself, the wound became infected and blood poisoning set in; it took emergency treatment in London to save his life, and one of his fingers had to be amputated.

Naturally he had no chance of taking part in the Cup. Without him, the Americans edged out Australasia in Wales, but lost 5-0 to Britain in the challenge round and didn't regain the trophy till 1913, by which time Beals C was no longer in the team.

After the 1906 brainstorm, a sympathetic All England Club presented him with a gold cigarette case. A bottle opener (or Swiss army toothbrush) might have been more to the point.

Before John Traicos started playing Test cricket for Zimbabwe in 1992, 22 years after being capped by South Africa, the longest gap in any player's Test career had been self-induced.

After scoring 52 and 61 at Sydney to help England win the final Test by 70 runs and the famous 1911–12 series 4-1, little George Gunn was given an envelope which he put in his jacket pocket and forgot about.

Not the way to make friends and influence people. The letter was from the England selectors, who, thinking they'd been snubbed, left him out for very nearly 18 years, until the 1929–30 tour of the West Indies, where he retained enough of his impish genius to score 85 and 47 in the last Test at the age of fifty.

John Snagge, for many years the BBC commentator on the university Boat Race ('I don't know who's in front, either Oxford or Cambridge') had been a student at Oxford. When the Dark Blues at last won the race again in 1937, Snagge was so engrossed in celebrating the end of the 14-year wait by pumping the hands

Foot in mouth
"Nichol never gives more than 120%."
KEVIN KEEGAN

of the Oxford rowers that he didn't look where he was going and walked too close to a lorry, which ran over his foot and broke a bone.

Just over six weeks after Roger Bannister had beaten him to the sub four minute barrier in the mile, John Landy of Australia took 1.4 seconds off the new world record to set up the winner-take-all race at the 1954 Commonwealth Games.

With opinions split between Landy's pace-setting and the Bannister finishing kick, the outcome was effectively settled the day before the final, when the Australian trod on a photographer's light bulb and gashed his foot so badly it needed four stitches. Bannister beat him by five yards.

Silvio Leonard, one of the warmest favourites for the 1976 Olympic 100 metre title, was injury-prone. To say the least. The previous year, he'd come through with a rush to steal the Pan-American title from Hasely Crawford of Trinidad – before falling into the moat surrounding the track.

While fooling around ten days before the Olympics, he stepped on a cologne bottle, broke it underfoot, and gashed his instep. He didn't reach the semi-finals, Crawford took the gold.

Four years later, slightly past his best, he clocked exactly the same time as Allan Wells (10.25, the slowest in an Olympic final since 1960) but was given only the silver medal.

During the fifth Test of the 1974–75 Ashes series, Jeff Thomson's assault on the England batsmen brought him his 33rd wicket, just three short of Arthur Mailey's 1920–21 record for a series against England. With the whole of the second innings to come, and another Test to follow, Thommo's chances of breaking the record were fairer than dinkum.

He didn't bowl in that second innings, and didn't play in the sixth Test. On the rest day of the fifth, he'd torn muscle fibres in his right shoulder while playing tennis. Mailey's record was broken by Rodney Hogg in 1978–79.

Hogg's total of 41 was itself overhauled two years later when Terry Alderman took 42 in the 1981 Ashes series. On England's 1982–83 tour to Australia, Alderman's chances of approaching that total were ended by another self-inflicted shoulder injury. Same side of the body, too.

When England passed 400 in their first innings of the first Test, fifteen spectators ran onto the pitch to celebrate. One of them seemed to give Alderman a clip round the ear (perhaps for having taken no more than one wicket in the innings) and was rugby-tackled by the medium-pacer in return.

A costly retaliation. Alderman dislocated his right shoulder, which was quickly reset but not restored. He couldn't bowl in the second innings, didn't play again in the series, and had to write the whole season off. Without him, Australia still won 2–1.

More than six years later, they won 4–0 in England, this time with Alderman doing his bit. Or rather his lot. He took 41 wickets in the six Tests to become the only bowler ever to twice take more than 34 in a series.

Three riders have won the Tour de France a record five times each: Jacques Anquetil, Eddy Merckx and Bernard Hinault. All three missed good chances of winning a sixth, Merckx in the most original way of all.

After his fifth win in 1974, fast Eddie was still suffering the after-effects of tonsilitis when he finished second to Bernard Thevenet the following year, and was installed as favourite yet again for 1976.

In the Giro d'Italia just a month or so before the Tour, he was hampered by a saddle sore which presented him with a choice: carry on in pain, in a race he couldn't win, or abandon it, have the boil lanced, and give himself three weeks to recover for the Tour. Merckx being Merckx, he went on to the bitter end, exacerbated the problem, and couldn't compete in France, missing out on a quite possible sixth win because of a boil on the bum.

The US boycott of the 1980 Olympics deprived Greg Louganis of a certain gold medal in the diving, but he made up for it in 1984 and 1988, becoming the only man to twice win the highboard and springboard titles at the same Olympics. Did it the hard way, too: needing an enormous 85.56 points on his last dive to win the 1988 highboard, he made it by 1.14. Earlier, he'd done himself no favours during the springboard preliminaries.

No diver goes through a career without a bit of bovver from board and water. The great Greg was no exception: two black eyes and a bloody nose after hitting a platform in 1976; knocked unconscious in 1979; broken collarbone in 1981.

Here in Seoul, he didn't push off far enough at the start of his ninth dive, came floating down on his back, and smacked his head on the board (a TV sequence that never fails to bring out the winces). Instead of a reverse two-and-a-half somersault, he landed like a side of ham.

Right: *Greg Louganis wins Olympic gold with a plaster on his scalp, but it's not a patch on his earlier dive* (Popperfoto)

Getting back on the horse that threw him, he chose another difficult dive, scored 87.12, qualified for the final, had five stitches and a waterproof patch applied to his scalp, and beat Tan Liang De of China into second place for the second successive Games.

If any further proof were needed that goalkeepers are one finger short of a full glove, Chris Woods provided it in early 1990. David Seaman won his third England cap, against Czechoslovakia at Wembley, after Woods had cut his hand with a penknife while wrestling with the waistband of his tracksuit bottoms – which proves the species is brave as well as bananas: anyone who wields a penknife in the vicinity of his trousers isn't short of balls. So to speak.

Mike Tereui, a weightlifter from the Cook Islands, took part in the 1990 Commonwealth Games, but his chances of success were limited by a broken hand, the result of the punch he'd thrown at a pig that raided his vegetable patch.

In 1984, Burrough Hill Lad sealed his greatest season (wins in the Hennessey Gold Cup and King George VI Chase) by taking the Cheltenham Gold Cup, which he had to miss the following year as the result of an injury in training: carrying his head very low in that unique way of his, he cut his knee with his own teeth!

In 1991, Scottish sprinter Euan Clarke cut his eyeball while trying to wipe the sweat off his forehead – with a crisp packet! The mind's eye boggles.

That same year, another Scotsman, Willie McBrinn, a magician who doubled as the British Over-60 Marathon champion, tried to combine the two activities by pulling a rabbit out of a hat while running – and injured himself by falling over a fence.

Dutch speed skater Yvonne van Gennip did her best to get into the Hall of Blame in 1988, spending a fortnight in hospital after cutting her right foot by tying the lace of her skating boot too tightly!

Good effort, but at the Winter Olympics soon afterwards she won three gold medals.

PRIDE COMETH . . .

In 1887–88 Preston North End were the best team in the country, champions in everything but name (champions in name too when they won the first ever League titles in the next two seasons) and dripping with great players: Nick and Jimmy Ross, John Goodall the best ball-player in England, Fred Dewhurst who scored 12 goals in 9 internationals, and three big Bobs: Mills-Roberts, Howarth, Holmes. Fearsome stuff on those mud pitches.

So confident were they of winning the FA Cup final that season (against West Brom, who'd lost the previous two finals without scoring a goal) that they apparently asked to be photographed with the cup *before* the match. The referee, Francis Marindin, suggested drily that they go through the formality of actually playing the game first. Preston lost 2-1.

In 1894, even without their famous England centre-forward GO Smith, the Old Carthusians won the first Amateur Cup final – so when Smith was available for the final the following year, they were heavily fancied to keep the prize, especially as five of the team were internationals: Leonard Rodwell Wilkinson in goal, the full-back brothers Arthur and Percy Walters, Hugh Stanbrough on the wing, and Gilbert Oswald Smith himself, a thin asthmatic ball-player who shot weakly but led a line well. Another international, Charles Wreford Brown, was missing.

The opposition, Middlesbrough, had none (though little Tommy Morren was to win a single England cap in 1898), reached the final by beating a very weak King's Own Lancashire Regiment, and generally looked eminently beatable.

Certainly the Old Boys thought so: the *North-Eastern Daily Gazette* confirms that they didn't bother taking the trophy north for the final at Headingley, where a last-minute header by Nelmes, following a corner, won Middlesbrough the cup, which they received some time later.

In 1897, the Scottish rugby union were so confident of retaining the Calcutta Cup that they didn't bring it down to Manchester with them. England won 12-3.

During the First World War, Louis Phal (which wasn't his real name), a Senegalese made to fight for France, won the *Croix de Guerre* for single-handedly wiping out a German machine-gun post. After the war, now calling himself Battling Siki, he did much the same to his opponents in the ring, his whirlwind style winning 49 out of 57 fights to earn a shot at the world light-heavyweight title held by the darling of France, the glamorous Georges Carpentier.

A grand stylist and knockout puncher, Carpentier was the overwhelming favourite, especially when he put Siki down in the first round. But then, to keep the crowd amused, gorgeous

Foot in mouth

"Perry Groves scored that Arsenal goal three minutes before the first half."
MIKE INGHAM

172

Georges began to toy with the underdog, who turned round and savaged him. By the sixth round, Carpentier was lying in a bloody heap and the division had its first black champion.

It seems to have gone to Siki's head: he took to walking through New York with a lion cub on a chain, shooting pistols in the streets, drinking too much. In 1923, six months after winning the title, disdainfully confident, he made the mistake of agreeing to defend it against an Irishman, in Dublin, on St Patrick's Night, in the middle of the Irish Rebellion.

Unaccustomed to having a nose thumbed at them so blatantly, the Fates punched it for him. In the last world title fight to go more than 15 rounds, he took a battering from Mike McTigue, who won by a mile on points.

In the final of the 1932 Olympic 800 metres, Alex Wilson of Canada tracked his team mate Phil Edwards through a suicidally fast first lap before passing him in the home straight.

Only a yard from the finish, Wilson threw both arms up in triumph – which allowed the bespectacled British schoolteacher Tommy Hampson to lunge past him on the line. Wilson finished five yards faster than the previous world record, but Hampson set a new one that lasted four years. Wilson won three Olympic medals but never a gold.

At the end of a race in Spain in 1991, British cyclist Malcolm Elliott held up both arms to acclaim his victory – and was passed by two other riders just before the line.

The legendary Tazio Nuvolari was the greatest Italian racing driver before Alberto Ascari, possibly of all time – but even he was given little chance of winning the 1935 Nordschleife, the big race of the year. His Alfa Romeo Tipo B, three years out of date, was no match for the Mercedes and Auto Unions which had won 8 major races that year: it had far less power and needed longer pit stops. When Nuvolari had to pull in for a blocked pressure pump, that seemed to be the end of it.

But the brilliant driver overcame the recalcitrant vehicle. Nuvolari got the ancient Alfa to run rings round the less manoeuvrable works machines and won at his leisure.

German officials had been so confident of winning that they hadn't thought to provide sheet music for the Italian national anthem – whereupon Nuvolari added a V sign to victory by producing some from his own pocket. He always carried it with him. For luck, he said.

Having won five titles at the 1967 Pan-American Games, 18-year-old swimmer Mark Spitz came to the Mexico Olympics predicting a haul of six gold medals. He won two, both in relays, and finished last in one of his individual finals.

Four years later, he slipped quietly into Munich, made no predictions, and won his unique total of seven golds.

Before their 1940 championship game (the Superbowl of its day) the Washington Redskins' owner George Preston Marshall called their opponents the Chicago Bears cry-babies: 'When the going gets tough, the Bears quit.' They did, too – after beating the Redskins 73-0 (seventy-three nil), an NFL record.

When the Americans arrived for the 1946 Davis Cup challenge round in Australia, the team voted unanimously to replace the stylish baseliner Frank Parker with the more aggressive Ted Schroeder.

Many thought it a mistake, including the Melbourne Sun's Bob Schlesinger, runner-up in the Australian singles finals of 1924 and 1929: 'Before it was announced that Schroeder would be America's second singles representative, I felt confident that Australia would defeat America by three rubbers to two, but now there is a decided possibility that the final tally will be four rubbers to one in favour of Australia.'

Schroeder won the opening singles and helped Jack Kramer dominate the doubles (see EATING DISORDERS) as Australia lost 5-0, the worst defeat suffered by any defending country.

John Kelly jnr, son of the great American rower Jack Kelly (who won three Olympic golds in the 1920s) and brother of Princess Grace of Monaco, took part in four Olympic Games. In 1950 Jack was so sure his son would beat Mervyn Wood of Australia in the Philadelphia Challenge Cup that he organised a victory ball before the final. Wood won the race.

Foot in mouth

"The day is coming when Rangers will be looking over their shoulder and wondering how Celtic got so far ahead."
TERRY CASSIDY

Ben Hogan was the leading golfer of his day, winner of nine Majors, including three out of four in 1953 (he couldn't compete in the USPGA). In 1955 he seemed to have won the US Open for the fifth time by shooting a last round 70 for a total of 287 with none of the other top players within range.

As he left the last green he handed his ball to the USPGA's executive secretary Joe Dey, telling him it was for Golf House, the USPGA headquarters and museum: here, have the ball which Ben

Hogan used to win a record fifth Open.

Behind him, Jack Fleck – a complete outsider who once claimed he 'couldn't putt into a tub' – scored 67, tied for the lead, and won the play-off by three strokes. Hogan never won another Major.

After the West Indies lost the 1975–76 Test series in Australia 5-1, England captain Tony Greig felt it safe enough to go on television and explain that when Caribbean teams were under pressure they grovelled and that England intended to make them do just that.

Even allowing for the pressures of talking into a microphone, and the fact that he might not have found the word he was looking for, it was an unthinking thing to say, especially for a white South African. Greig was bowled for a duck in his first innings of the series, scored a brave 116 and 76 not out in the fourth Test but averaged 7.28 in the others, and took only 5 wickets at 67.20 each as England lost the series 3-0 and didn't win another Test against the West Indies till 1990.

Before his comeback title fight at Madison Square Garden in 1971, Muhammad Ali was as demure as ever: 'Frazier's got two chances: slim and none.' Smokin' Joe knocked him down in the last round and won easily on points.

Left: *The leg stump grovels. AW Greig, b. Holding, 1. Last day, last Test, 1976.*
(Popperfoto)

Even though more than a dozen of the best Australian cricketers had gone over to Packer, new Test captain Graham Yallop said he fancied winning the 1978–79 Ashes series 6-0. A full-strength England won it 5-1.

Despite his failure to win a medal at the 1971 European athletics championships, David Bedford's self-confidence, on the surface at least, was undented: 'The difference between me and other athletes is that they go to the Olympics to compete and I go to win.' He finished 6th in the 10000 metres (150 yards behind the winner) and 12th in the 5000 as Lasse Viren did his first double.

Before his world middleweight title defence against Marvin Hagler in 1980, Alan Minter vowed there was no way he was 'going to lose my title to no black man'. Hagler cut his eye, stopped him in three rounds, kept the title for more than six years, and never lost it to no white man.

'I don't think there's any arrogance there at all' – Steve Ovett on that habit he had of waving to the crowd after taking the lead in the homestretch. Wave the other one, Steve.

The gesture, which got under other runners' skins, brought in the crowds, who were rewarded for their patience a week after the 1980 Olympics.

Ovett's first race since losing the Moscow 1500m to Coe was a 5000 in the IAC meeting at Crystal Palace. Coming into the straight, he kicked past John Treacy of Ireland, a strong runner not known for his finish (world cross-country champion 1978 and 1979, Olympic Marathon silver medallist 1984). Out came the royal wave, up went the roar of the crowd.

They'd seen what Ovett hadn't, that Treacy had come again: dipping at the line, he reached it a fraction in front (they shared the same time of 13:27.9). Apart from the 1986 Commonwealth 5000 against a weakened field (another African boycott), Ovett didn't win another major title.

After St Helens had beaten Wigan in the 1966 rugby league Challenge Cup final, Saints' Alex Murphy sent a telegram to the losers' HQ: 'Roses are red, violets are blue, St Helens 21, Wigan 2.' Payback took 23 years. In the 1989 final, all-conquering Wigan beat St Helens (now coached by Murphy) 27-0.

PROPHETS AND THEIR LOSSES

Harry Brown was a leading jockey who also had the ear of the Prince of Wales. When the future Edward VIII thought of betting on the 100-6 shot Sergeant Murphy in the 1923 Grand National, Brown wasn't keen: 'Good god, no. He's as old as I am. He's not a horse at all.'

While Sergeant Murphy was winning the National easily, Harry Brown was making himself scarce in one of the champagne bars.

James Rank, 30 years an owner, had the usual ambitions in racing: to win the Derby and Grand National. When he died in 1952 he'd spent a fortune but won neither. Although he owned the 1946 Cheltenham Gold Cup winner Prince Regent, the nearest he got to the National was when he had the chance to buy a young horse that a friend thought would never be a champion. Rank kept his hand in his pocket.

The horse, Reynoldstown, won the Grand National in 1935 and 1936 (see BLASTED CONTRAPTIONS).

Gordon Richards, winner of the jockey's title 26 times, didn't give a young man called Piggott much chance of winning his first, in 1960: 'If only Lester were seven pounds lighter he would certainly top the jockeys' list. As it is, I very much doubt . . .' Piggott went on to win the first of his 11 titles.

Richards could take comfort from the racing correspondent who wrote in 1954 that 'Lester Piggott, who is now 18, is still growing and it may well be that he has ridden his last race on the Flat. Next season I expect him to turn to jumping in which weight is less important.'

Great Britain, who'd won the inaugural rugby league World Cup (1954), were heavy favourites to win the second (1957 in Australia), at least as far as commentator Eddie Waring was concerned:

'It's hardly worth paying the cost of the big trophy by taking it to Sydney. It should be so easy for Britain to win with a side like

Foot in mouth
"I never predict anything and I never will do."
PAUL GASCOIGNE

Dennis Lillee and Jeff Thomson mauled England throughout the 1974–75 series, bowling Australia to wins in four of the first five Tests – but then Thomson was injured before the sixth (see WHO NEEDS FRIENDS . . ?) and Lillee during it. In their absence, England's batsmen put together 529 (the shell-shocked captain Denness 188, Keith Fletcher 146) to take a first-innings lead of 377.

Australia reached the end of the third day with all ten second innings wickets standing. When they ended the fourth 103 behind with seven wickets left, the Melbourne Sun printed the headline WE'VE SAVED IT.

England won by an innings.

this against the sort of team Australia can field.'

The Kangaroos beat Britain 30-6 on the way to winning the Cup.

Cyril Knowles, the Tottenham Hotspur and England full-back, had an even more talented brother Peter, a stylish midfielder capped at youth and under-23 level before suddenly dropping out of League football to become a Jehovah's Witness in 1969.

He had to. He didn't have much time left. 'We believe the world will end in 1975. If you study the Bible, it'll tell you.' The number of Bibles printed since 1975 runs into many millions.

When the Faeroe Islands were granted membership of FIFA in 1988, the earth didn't shatter. When they entered the next European Championship, maps were hurriedly consulted in search of this huddle of rocky islands in the middle of the North Atlantic (the national team had once been lost in a storm for 24 hours), with a population of 45000, parliament of six MPs, dependence on fish, and not a grass pitch in sight: their first ever competitive fixture, a home game against Austria, had to be moved to Landskrona in Sweden.

The Austrians weren't the best team in Europe themselves. Disappointing in the 1990 World Cup finals, they had a very average defence and seemed to lack leadership on and off the pitch. Still, their strikers Toni Polster and Gerhard Rodax had cost Spanish clubs £5 million between them, and predictions of 4-0 and 5-0 sounded conservative.

Against this size of fee, the Faeroese put out the traditional amateur pick'n'mix: a dentist's manager moonlighting as a folk singer (the captain Joannes Jakobsen), a baker, carpenter, bank clerk, fishmonger (naturally), car salesman, assorted students. Their ambition, they said: to keep the score down. Long term: to become as good as Finland within five years. No wonder one of their own journalists agreed to walk all the way home if they avoided defeat.

By half-time, goalkeeper Jens Martin Knudsen had made his knitted hat famous with a number of fine saves. After 63 minutes, Torkil Nielsen had gone through the middle to score. The defence held out to the end: the biggest upset in European Championship history.

Austria's manager Josef Hickersberger resigned, the Faeroes went on to draw 1-1 in Belfast, and the journalist of little faith honoured his bet by walking home. Thirty miles. In the nude.

WRITING WRONGS

mistakes in print

Daily Telegraph 1978: 'Javed Miandad was the eighth to go. He was stretched well forward when a ball from Doshi raped him on the pad.'

Lusty bowlers, these Indians. The Telegraph again: 'In the collapse after the interval, the 26-year-old Prasanna shot out seven batsmen for 69 runs in 16 lovers, two of which were maidens.'

The highest individual score ever made in a Test match is Brian Lara's 375 against England in 1994, but Reuters begged to differ many years earlier. Their scorecard for England's first innings at Johannesburg in 1938:

PA Gibb	not out	559
E Paynter	not out	1009
Extras		5

Paul Gibb actually made 93, Eddie Paynter 117, extras 10, England 422. Match drawn.

Below: *Javed Miandad enjoying the attentions of Dilip Doshi, a true cricket lover* (Allsport/Adrian Murrell)

Jack Nicklaus' name isn't exactly unknown in his field – but the scoreboard at the 1973 British Open wasn't always sure: at one stage, it took his name and Bert Yancey's, cut them in half, and put them back together to announce an unknown but distinctly promising newcomer, Nickey Yanclaus.

Arnold Palmer retained his British Open title in 1961 by a single stroke after a famous shot on the 16th. Having pushed his tee shot into heavy rough (some say a small bush), he could have played safe with a wedge, but wouldn't have been Arnie if he hadn't gone for broke with a 6 iron.

Thrashing at the ball so hard that he ripped the bush out of the ground, he reached the green 140 yards away and saved his par.

A plaque at Royal Birkdale commemorates the shot, only the second to have been put up to a player on a British Open course. It reads, quite simply: 'Arnold Palmer, The Open Championship, 14th July 1961'.

Fine. Good old British understatement. Except that virtually all play was abandoned on the 14th July, which Palmer spent playing bridge while waiting for conditions to improve. His famous shot was played on Saturday the 15th.

The first three AAA 100 yard sprints were won by WP (William Page) Phillips, a giant by the standards of the day (1880–81–82) at 6ft 2½in and 12st 2lb, who also set the first official British record over 220 yards: 22.0 in 1878.

When his death was announced just two years after his last AAA success, Phillips felt moved to write in from abroad and let it be known that he was alive and in good health.

Embarrassment for the newspaper involved – but tempting of fate by Phillips: he died just four months later, aged 25.

For their match at Murrayfield in 1929, the French rugby team broke new ground by wearing numbered jerseys. About time too. But not much use to spectators. The numbers hadn't been printed in the match programme!

Foot in mouth

"Kiptanui, the 19-year-old turned 20 a few weeks ago."
DAVID COLEMAN

In March 1952, two months after world heavyweight champion Jersey Joe Walcott boxed a series of exhibitions in Maine, his main challenger Rocky Marciano followed suit.

The Associated Press described Rocky's first demonstration, in Lewiston, as 'a power exhibition in a four-round sparring duel with amateur Peter Fuller of Boston'. Marciano looked the part, but 'the unawed Fuller, son of a former Massachusetts governor, gave a satisfactory show and drew a respectable round of applause'.

Three nights later, the two fighters sparred in Rumford, then in other towns across the state, the press giving Marciano's opponent fulsome notices: usually Fuller, occasionally another amateur Tony Zullo.

There was just one thing. Fuller, worried that fighting a professional might rule him out of contention for the Olympics, had stayed at home. So had Zullo. The boxer Marciano fought in every one of those exhibitions was his own brother Sonny!

When publishers Nicholas Kaye brought out Gardnar Mulloy's autobiography just before Wimbledon in 1959, the blurb on the dust jacket announced that 'there is no doubt in anyone's mind that he is one of the three best players of amateur status in the world today' and that 'the character of this young American player shines with honesty and forthrightness.'

One of the top three? With Laver, Fraser, Olmedo and Emerson around? Well alright let's call it a matter of opinion. Honesty and forthrightness? Yep, plenty of that: Gardnar Putnam Mulloy had always been his own man. Young? Well, at heart maybe. Mulloy was 45!

Gardnar Mulloy was habitually at loggerheads with the tennis authorities, especially old sticklers like Norman Brookes. A mischievous talented strokeplayer just below the highest class, Mulloy might have won the Wimbledon singles title if there hadn't been so many other good Americans around at the same time.

He would have had his best chance in 1949 if one of those, Ted Schroeder, hadn't deigned to enter. Just before the championships, Mulloy let it be known that he thought the draw for the singles was fixed.

His tongue was firmly in his cheek, and the seedings committee knew it, but they entered into the spirit of the thing by inviting him to make the draw himself, an offer he couldn't be seen to resist.

Mulloy, who'd just missed being seeded, pulled his own name out of the bag last of all, drawing himself against the No. 1 seed and favourite Schroeder, who beat him from two sets down and went on to win the championship at his only attempt.

The irrepressible Mulloy won his only Wimbledon title, a hugely popular success in the 1957 doubles, at the age of 43.

Record books used to list two players called Hunte as having played Test cricket for the West Indies in the 1930s – RL once, EAC twice – until it was realised that 'RL' was simply a copy typist's version of Errol, who won all the three caps!

Foot in mouth
"I was 18 about six years ago. I'm 28 now."
FRANK BRUNO

INDEX

182